INSIDE THE FENCE

Inside the Fence

A Handbook for Those in Prison Ministry

REV. DAVID M. SCHILDER

ALBA·HOUSE NEW YORK
SOCIETY OF ST. PAUL, 2187 VICTORY BLVD., STATEN ISLAND, NEW YORK 1031

ST PAULS

Library of Congress Cataloging-in-Publication Data

Schilder, David M.
    Inside the Fence: a handbook for those in prison ministry / David M.
    Schilder.
        p.   cm.
    ISBN 0-8189-0855-6
    1. Church work with prisoners.   2. Prison chaplains.   I. Title.
    BV4340.S35   1999
    259'.5—dc21   98-47270
                                                            CIP

Produced and designed in the United States of America by the
Fathers and Brothers of the Society of St. Paul,
2187 Victory Boulevard, Staten Island, New York 10314,
as part of their communications apostolate.

ISBN: 0-8189-0855-6

Printing Information:

Current Printing - first digit   1   2   3   4   5   6   7   8   9   10

Year of Current Printing - first year shown

1999   2000   2001   2002   2003   2004   2005

TABLE OF CONTENTS

FOREWORD

by Reverend Josiah Opata, Chaplain, M.A.C.I.

Reverend David M. Schilder is an ordained Roman Catholic priest. He served as a chaplain at the Orient Correctional Institution in Orient, Ohio. In his eighteen years of experience as an institutional chaplain, he has trained several chaplains, including Catholics, Muslims, Native Americans, Wiccans, Jews and others. He is very ecumenical and unique in his service to "the least of our brethren experiencing problems in living."

Father Dave, as we affectionately call him, says a correctional chaplain serves the church and society in an appointment beyond the local church. He/she is the bridge between the religious groups represented in the prison and those in society. As such, every effort is made by the correctional chaplain to train pastors of all denominations, or at least to provide them with the resource materials needed to make these pastors more effective ministers. *Inside the Fence* is just such a resource — a must book for all professional correctional ministers or would-be chaplains.

We must be secure in our own faith journeys if we are not to feel threatened by other faiths different from our own. We must continuously further our education and spirituality in order to be effective pastoral care providers. Chaplaincy is a skill that takes several years in seminary, church or congregational life and clinical practice to develop. It may seem easy from the outside, but like other professions it is a skilled occupation not to be taken lightly by politicians and administrators. Entertainment preaching is not to be compared with chaplaincy work. It is a dedicated, courageous and enduring job to be performed.

The goal of chaplaincy is to help both staff members and inmates to mature in their stages of faith. Through education, the chaplain contributes to the propagation of truth — in receiving and dispensing of religious information. So the chaplain provides a listening ear, a resource library of information, and a viable center for all faiths to develop and to grow.

The chaplain, like a poet, can master the art of prose so as to use the five senses of touch, smell, hearing, vision and taste for all to experience the reality of the Almighty experienced in nature. He/she is like a lyricist, using all the beauty of creation to speak to the human condition and the goal of life. It is alright to borrow religious symbols, rituals and even clothing that are not available in one's own endorsing church if it helps our congregants to get in touch with themselves spiritually and emotionally, in order to give them a high sense of self-esteem. We must read widely from all cultures, all traditions and across racial barriers to equip us to minister to all faiths. Chaplaincy has no room for shallowness and intolerance.

With one chaplain serving an average of about 1,500 inmates in Ohio, the need for volunteers cannot be undervalued. They provide such invaluable services, including spiritual resources, after-care, bible studies, ministers of record who provide pastoral care, lead worship services and so on. A chaplain may spend part or all of his or her day off recruiting and training volunteers, in speaking engagements, attending seminars and conferences as a participant or as featured speaker, and in media interviews, among other things, all of which are far beyond the chaplain's call of duty. In North Carolina, the governor's office has a full-time volunteer coordinator who sees to it that all volunteers are recognized and rewarded every year for their invaluable services.

This book is a must for correctional administrators and politicians who legislate corrections, as well as church administrators and seminary deans.

AUTHOR'S NOTE

The following is strictly one person's opinion. It is not written in response to any particular central office policy, administrator, group of chaplains or otherwise. Nor is it my intention to imply that this is the last word on the subject. Rather, it is intended as a starter for further discussions on what a chaplain is in the corrections system. Since there has been a dearth of written material and references on the role of the chaplain, it is my hope that this material will lead to an exchange of ideas in the formal arena. Then, perhaps we might be able to develop a better and stronger chaplaincy that can function in an ever more professional manner for the inmates we were hired to serve.

Also, I hope that administrative personnel might benefit from this dialogue so that they may understand and utilize more fully the skills and services a chaplain has to offer them.

Finally, in the Epilogue, in an attempt to help you understand why I feel I am qualified to make and state some of the following positions and philosophies, I am including a resume of my educational, professional and life experiences.

PROLOGUE

Jesus began to speak to the crowds about John: "What did you go out to the wasteland to see — a reed swaying in the wind? Tell me, what did you go out to see — someone luxuriously dressed? Remember, those dressed luxuriously are to be found in royal palaces. Why then did you go out — to see a prophet? A prophet indeed, and something more!" (Matthew 11:7)

Many times I have thought this passage could be rewritten *for chaplains and administrators* of prisons to read in the following manner.

For chaplains:

"What did you get ordained to be — receivers of public adulation and performers in a sanctuary as though on a stage? Tell me, what did you get ordained to be — someone who is well paid and well respected, someone who is waited on hand and foot? Remember, those who are well paid and well respected and waited on hand and foot are to be found in the clutches of the power brokers of a humanistic and materialistic culture. Why then did you get ordained — to to be a servant? A servant indeed, and much more!"

For administrators:

"What did you hire a chaplain to be — a pious preacher of pablum from Sunday pulpits? Tell me, what did you hire a chaplain to be — someone to decorate your table of organization in order to satisfy the desires of politicians and do-gooders to have a nebulous religious presence in the prison? Remember, those who are phonies have no conscience and weigh less than a feather on the scale of morality. Why then did you hire a chaplain — to provide religious nourishment and leadership for hurting human beings? A religious leader indeed, and so much more!"

INSIDE THE FENCE

CHAPTER ONE

THE CHAPLAIN AS SERVANT

The chaplain is a *public servant who works for the inmates on behalf of the religious community in cooperation with the government.* Before a further explanation is given, an analogy is in order. A surgeon, another member of the original set of professions (religion, medicine and law) provides his highly-trained skills for the inmates under the license of those who trained him for his profession in cooperation with the state for whom the inmate is a ward. The government provides the physical setting, with all of its equipment and supplies, in order that the surgeon may deliver to the inmates the skills for which he was trained. Now, let us return to the original sentence to review what it means in the context of chaplaincy.

Public:

The chaplain works outside the property or territorial domain of the church, just as the surgeon or doctor works outside the private domain of the community or private hospital. In working for wards of society in a government institution, the chaplain is salaried by the state in accordance with commensurate and comparable pay scales and benefits in the profession, if the work were performed in a church setting. The hours of work

1

and the work place are established by the government, comparable to hours, work site, staff, equipment and supplies, if the work were performed in a church setting.

Servant:

The chaplain offers the fruit of the skills and knowledge he has earned under the extensive tutelage of other licensed and skilled masters of the profession. In the finest tradition of the profession of translating the truths about man's relationship with God, the chaplain as servant freely and responsively ministers to the inmates. Since his profession, in the teachings of all the major religions of the world, always speaks up for the rights of the individual person against injustices wrought against the individual person by private persons or governmental agencies, he will not permit his person or profession to be used and abused. To allow a government agent to tell him how to function as a professional, would be a personal and professional abuse. Only those who are licensed, skilled, and experienced as ordained chaplains may stand in judgment of the chaplain's professional performance. Just as a warden or deputy warden would not think of telling a surgeon how to perform an appendectomy, it is just as unthinkable for them to tell a chaplain how to be a pastor.

However, the state may hire other qualified and well-experienced clergy persons to supervise the professional performance of a chaplain, just as it may hire the supervisory skills of a medical board of review.

A servant is not a slave. When a chaplain permits himself to be directed in pastoral matters by a warden or a deputy warden, the whole notion of servanthood is obliterated and slavery exists just as surely as a serf was a slave of the lord of the manor.

While there is a degree of servanthood to the civilian personnel in a prison, the chaplain's primary role of servant is lived out in a relationship to the inmate. It is the inmates' needs for which the chaplain is hired. Civilian personnel have access to all of the denominations in their home communities. Thus, a chaplain sets his hours of ministry to be most available to the inmates when they are free from lockup and most work assignments. Accordingly, he makes a professional judgment and analysis of the needs of the inmates and provides those worship and religious education services the inmates need and can comprehend. The chaplain's own desires and religious tastes or expressions are subordinated to the cultural spiritual expressions of the inmates.

Just as the warden is a public servant, and it would be totally inappropriate for him to act or behave in a manor that would give the message that he expects to be publicly served, so the chaplain as public servant schedules staff meetings, research work, correspondence, record keeping and workshops at times when the inmates have the least access to the Religious Services Center and its staff. That is not, or should not be, a unique servanthood role to administrators and department heads within the prison system. We are all hired to serve the inmates; not one another.

In the religious tradition that says the servant should not be greater than the master, the chaplain as servant must not be greater than the master, the chaplain as servant must not be present to the inmates in any manner or style that implies a "better state." All mannerisms or lifestyles or types of dress that imply a superior/inferior relationship or identify with the hedonism of materialism are out of order. For example, one inmate was heard talking to another inmate about the chaplains of a prison where the inmate used to be. He said he had worked for both chaplains and that one of them treated him like a slave, while the other treated him like an equal human being. A chaplain should never ask an inmate to do something for him that the chaplain wouldn't be willing to do for himself, if he had the time. The chaplain never takes on the institutional manners of speech where ordering people around is the custom rather than customary courtesies that express respect.

It is never appropriate for a chaplain to wear custom-tailored suits or large displays of gold jewelry or sixty-dollar-an-ounce after shave lotions. To preach the eternal verities of the spiritual life and to present oneself at the same time as identified with the worst of conspicuous consumption in this age is a complete contradiction in body language. The inmates will not miss the message. While the inmates want their religious leaders to dress respectably and not look like tramps — after all, the chaplain is a professional — they really prefer that the chaplain dress humbly and decently. I am not saying that a chaplain should imitate an inmate's uniform. On the other hand, neither should the chaplain look like an advertisement for *Gentlemen's Quarterly*.

Who works for the inmates:

The bottom line is that the chaplain works for the inmates. While the legal hiring authority, as far as the state is concerned, is the warden, the chaplain does not work for the warden. She works for the inmates and with the warden. She works with the warden in all that is legal, moral and just. That distinction must never be breached or the chaplain is not a chaplain. The moment she takes orders from the warden, she becomes nothing more or less than a civilian and completely loses her role as a professional.

By the same token, a chaplain must give due respect to where it is she is working and the primary purpose of the facility in which she is working. Following due process, the courts have decided that the inmates need to be separated from society. The first order of business, then, for the institution, is to maintain that separation.

The law stipulates that a person is sent to prison *as* punishment, not *for* punishment. The implied purposes of the laws in setting lengths of time for the incarceration are twofold. The first is that the inmate will come back to society having paid some debt for her wrong. The second is that she return to society as a changed and morally sound person as a direct result of her incarceration.

Thus, the chaplain respects the warden's need for a secure and orderly operated institution. The chaplain will follow administrative regulations. If it is her professional judgment that any of the regulations are unjust, she will work in a responsible manner to see that those rules are changed. She will work through the ordinary chains of command, out of respect for those in civil authority, unless those in the chain of authority become a stumbling block to creative and responsible change, or unless they are functioning in an immoral or unjust manner.

While the chaplain strives to respect those in authority, as the basic tenets of the major religions teach, she also must answer to a higher authority, as the major religions also teach, when people are being hurt, used or abused.

It is the responsibility of the chaplain to know who her people are. She needs to know their educational levels of achievement. She needs to know the emotional levels at which most of them are functioning. Finally, by all means, she needs to know the levels of their spiritual growth and the stages of their faith development.

As a servant working for the inmates, she must not only be behind them pushing them on to greater levels of growth and a more mature, responsible expression of lived faith, she must be a leader. But she must not be so far ahead of them that she loses them. There is Paul's "So am I" (2 Cor 11:22) that comes to mind, and his statement about feeding people at the various stages where you find them (1 Cor 3:1-2). Thus, a chaplain must be conversant in all the latest technical and scholarly spiritual terms. She must have absorbed them into her lived spirituality. But, above all she must be able to relate those terms in a language that her people will understand and to the level of development she is called to lead them. Answering the call to inspire people to practice their faith, she is like a spiritual cheerleader. She has to be willing to be seen as a person who lives out her faith amidst the struggles of life that confront all people.

On a practical level, the chaplain must recognize and accept as appropriately useful the various cultural expressions of faith, even though they might not be her original heritage. Because the chaplain did not grow up in a spiritual environment that included expressive hand and body movements or sang music in other than a Western mode, she must be supportive of the spiritual values of those other expressions. The same is true if she did not grow up in a faith with a predominantly liturgical expression. To disdain or thwart those communal worship styles in any manner is to lose sight of who it is the chaplain is working for and where it is she wishes to lead them. To be effective as a spiritual leader the chaplain must learn to identify with all the prayer forms of her parishioners.

In summary, just as the surgeon does not work for the warden, she must never forget that her skills are given her for the services of her patients and not the puffing up of her personality or her personal material aggrandizement. While she cooperatively works with the administration in those areas that do not violate the code of ethics for her profession, her independence must be maintained.

On behalf of the religious community:

A prison population of two thousand people may have as many as a dozen major faith groups represented and as many as fifty denominations within those faith groups. A prison population is also an ever-changing population, changing at a more rapid pace than most do on the streets.

Religious leaders in suburbia may experience as much as twenty-five percent of their congregation being involved in a geographical relocation each year. At the same time, because civilians tend to take their faith for granted, the spiritual growth of the members of the congregation may be almost imperceptible in the course of a year. It is not unusual for a chaplain to experience as much as a fifty percent geographical relocation of her congregation each year. On the other hand, because the members of her congregation are physically restricted, they have more time to look inward and upward. On average, compared to members of congregations in suburbia, the inmates' spiritual growth is more noticeable and taken more seriously.

While it is the responsibility of the state to guarantee the inmates the rights to worship publicly, it is a practical impossibility to provide a paid pastoral staff for each denomination within a major faith group. Thus when we speak of "the religious community," we are speaking of all major faith communities and, more specifically, those major faith communities to which the inmates will be returning after serving their sentences.

It is the responsibility and duty of the chaplain to know the major teachings of those faith groups. He should reach out to those major faith communities to seek authorized volunteers or recruit contractual persons to minister to those faith groups for which he is not a member. While a growing number of inmates will be in prison for more years than many members of the congregations in the civilian community, the chaplain is still appropriately the transitional pastor for them. In his role as a pastor, he must remember that he is their temporary spiritual guide and mentor. It is his role to lead them to that spiritual development which it is hoped they will maintain when they are released.

The chaplain must not only be in responsible communication with the leadership of his denomination, he must have the public relations ability to be in responsible communication with all the faith groups his people represent. He must strive to give each faith group as much time, space and equipment, supplies and materials for the development of their religious programs as he does for his own. Within his public relations responsibility, he must be conversant in the protocols of all the faiths represented in the prison.

On the practical side, when employees at any level of administration of the institution are discussing religion, religious practices, or religious policies, it is the chaplain who should be consulted. When a question of medical practice comes up among social workers, correctional officers or the warden, it would be recognized as highly inappropriate for them to issue policy regulations and procedures without consulting the doctor. Religious questions that affect the lives of inmates must always be decided with the consultation and direction of the chaplain, and the respectful following of his orders and decisions. It is part of the chaplain's role to be the resident theologian.

It is never appropriate for the warden's office or the deputy warden's office to be the first line of decision making, when a civilian clergyman calls with questions about religious practices in the prison. While the chaplain is not the expert on security matters, the warden and deputy wardens are not pastors. However, the pastors, wardens and deputy wardens must function in a manner that mutually affirms the roles of one another.

In cooperation with the government:

The best of religious traditions follows the basic teaching of giving to Caesar what is Caesar's and giving to God what is God's. If the government does its part by supplying adequate salaries, buildings and equipment, and the chaplain does her part in supplying professional pastoral care, society benefits by having returned to it a more responsible citizen. The key element here is the word "with." The chaplain never provides her ministry for the state. She works with the state in all that is legal, ethical, moral and just.

The following incident might help to illustrate some of the key points of this chapter. It occurred during an exchange of ideas I had with one of the ten wardens with whom I have worked.

The warden had received a written complaint from an inmate in which the inmate stated that I would not let him sing in the choir because he was gay. The inmate had told me, *not* under the seal of confession, that he was in an active relationship with another inmate. Using the principle that a pastor would not let an inebriated parishioner come to the pulpit to proclaim the scriptures or participate in the choir, I told the inmate, whose behavior was openly known to most men in his dormitory, that he could join the choir if he came to church every Sunday, participating as any other congregant, and abstained from his sexual relationship with the other inmate. His relationship with another man was not only found to be inappropriate behavior by almost every major religion in the world, but it was also against institutional policy.

The warden called me to his office to tell me that I must permit the inmate to sing in the choir. Assuring the warden that I was not denying the inmate his right to come to church and that there was a pastoral responsibility not to allow the man to give blatant scandal to the worshipping community, I respectfully told the warden that his decision was an interference in the principle of the separation of church and state.

In all fairness to the warden, he did not catch onto the other element that the inmate was openly admitting to a behavior that was forbidden in the institution. It was days later that the element registered with him.

But, at the moment, when I told him I would not follow his orders, he raised his voice and told me he ran the institution, and I would do as I was instructed. I responded by acknowledging his authority, but assured him that he did not run the religious services department, nor did he have the authority to step into or countermand a moral issue. He then stood up, leaned across the desk and pointed his finger at my face, saying in an even louder voice, "Listen, Bud, you better wake up and smell the roses." At that point I stood up, leaned across the desk, pointed my finger at his face, saying, "Listen, Bud, I work for the man who makes the roses."

After a pause, he laughed. We then continued the discussion for a few more minutes. The inmate was not permitted to sing in the choir. He was welcome to come to church and he did so. After a few months he discontinued his sexual relationship with the other inmate and was allowed to sing in the choir.

CHAPTER TWO

THE CHAPLAIN AS PRIEST

The chaplain is the *presider and originator of all worship services in the institution.* Following the earlier analogy a little further, the surgeon either performs the surgery as head of a team or he directs members of the surgical team to assist him in those areas he cannot do alone, or he directs others to learn his techniques in order that more surgery may be performed, and more people will have a chance at better health.

Presider:

The chaplain is the first presider at prayer and worship. He leads all those services for which there is no theological conflict with his denomination. He does not call upon a volunteer of his denomination to do what he could and should do first. He may call upon assistance when the number of services becomes too great to practically meet all the responsibilities.

If it is customary for a minister in his denomination to preside and preach at three worship services on a weekend, then he would be expected to do so within a prison setting. The chief common denominator is that what applies for the clergy as pastors of a congregation in civilian society should apply for the prison chaplain as pastor for the inmates. It is commonly expected by most religious congregations in civilian society that the pastor preside at the main worship service of that faith group each week, allowing for vacation leave and unforeseen sickness. The same standard should apply for the prison chaplain as pastor.

It is commonly accepted that eighty percent of a clergyman's parishioners will only see him on a regular basis at the main worship service of the week. Thus, his prime moment of ministry is at that time. It is observed that about the same percentages hold true in the prison setting. For that reason, the chaplain as a responsible pastor must be the presider at his faith group's main worship service of the week.

It has been objected that pastors of some congregations are bi-vocational. They hold two jobs in order to make a living. That practice is true for those congregations that do not have enough members to be able to afford the pastor a full-time salary. The prison chaplain, when he is hired by the state, is hired as a full-time employee. His salary and fringe benefits are adequate. He is paid to be the leader of public worship and public prayer. If the state wanted to hire a pastoral counselor or a coordinator of volunteer services, it could save money and hire part-time contractors for those services.

To finagle and manipulate the work schedule so that the chaplain presides at worship for his faith group every other week or less often is professionally unethical and probably immoral, because he is not fulfilling the duties understood as the main term of his employment, when he was hired. Every major religion expects its teacher/minister/pastor to be present to the congregation when it is time to worship.

In the Christian faith, there is a saying that, "You cannot serve two masters. You will either hate the one and love the other, or love the one and hate the other." You cannot serve a civilian congregation and a prison congregation at the same time. When there is time for a wedding, a funeral, or a parishioner is in the hospital, critically ill, who does the bi-vocational chaplain serve first? If he has a family in addition to the two congregations, whose needs can he meet? He only has so much energy. To which group is he going to play second fiddle?

If the chaplain truly understands himself to be a pastor, there will be a natural desire within him to want to be with a congregation of men, women and children at worship. He should have had that experience with a congregation in civilian society for at least three years before he answered the call to ministry in a prison setting. But it is precisely that call to prison ministry on a full-time basis that he answered when he received the endorsement from his denomination to be hired by the state as a full-time chaplain. It is definitely a sacrifice not to be with a civilian congregation, when a pastor works in a prison setting, but what kind of service is it that does not entail sacrifice?

If there are two chaplains of the same denomination or basic faith group serving in the same institution, when it comes to the celebration of the main worship service of the week, they can do one of two things. First, they could concelebrate the service, giving living witness to the inmates of a mutually-supportive ministry. While they could alternate preaching responsibilities, their witness of praying together could preach more about communal faith support than any fifty sermons. Secondly, they could alternate visiting those inmates, who are unable or unwilling to participate with the larger community at prayer. Each week whichever chaplain is not the main celebrant could simultaneously be visiting the sick — bringing them communion and anointing them, visiting those confined to isolated security cells, or making pastoral rounds in the dormitories. The chaplain, who is not the main celebrant for the week, should be spending that same prayer time in prayer with those who, for whatever reason, cannot be at the Religious Services Center.

The personal visit by the chaplain to those who have expressed a preference for a faith group, but who have not yet actively attended, will be a moment that inmate will never forget. Rather than calling him into the office, the chaplain should be concerned enough about the inmate to go out of his way to pray with him and attempt to discern the pain that keeps him from joining the community at prayer. The Christian example of Christ going out to find the one lost sheep should be example enough for the dedicated chaplain to justify this outreach ministry.

There is an old spiritual dictum, "Nemo dat quod non habet." Loosely translated, it means you can't give what you don't have. The leader of prayer cannot be a leader of prayer if she is not a person of prayer. She cannot be a leader of prayer, if she has not kept up with the insights and developments in the theological understanding of public prayer that her faith group expresses. In other words, the chaplain must spend some time every day in private prayer and spiritual reading. It is a long-standing spiritual recommendation of most denominations and most faith groups that at least one hour be set aside each day for this purpose. A personal devotional life is a prerequisite for any effective ministry, including corrections.

The negative side of this standard is that the state does not provide a structure whereby the chaplain can take an hour for herself to pray. Even if the state were to change its practices and procedures for the chaplain to be able to set aside one hour for private prayer and spiritual reading, the demands for pastoral services are already twice as great on the chaplain as they are on the average for a community clergy person.

Thus, the practical side of this issue is that the chaplain will have to take the time away from work each day to be able to perform as a spiritual leader at work. By the same token, a lay person working for the prison system, who is also committed to her faith life, will have to find time away from work to nourish her prayer life.

As a side note, a woman volunteer at the prison where I work gets up at 4:30 A.M. every day for prayer and spiritual reading before going to work in downtown Columbus. She is an active grandmother, a lay minister at her parish, visits the sick in the hospital two nights a week, and still finds time to spend every Saturday morning and afternoon ministering to inmates. While it is true that very few prison employees are expected to take work home with them, and even fewer are expected to do it seven days a week, the chaplain must see this "homework" of prayer as the absolutely most vital fuel that gives her energy to function inside the prison, while she is on the time clock. Some laity who are not ministers do as much.

It is also a requirement of most denominations and faith groups that their clergy in civilian communities renew themselves periodically in the spirituality of the faith group. This is commonly done by members of the clergy of the faith group by gathering in an isolated area for prayer and study, under the direction of a recognized spiritual authority of that faith group. Normally, one full week is usually required for such gatherings, or retreats as they are commonly called, to be effective. It is highly recommended that a pastor view such an annual experience as an absolute requirement for continued effective ministry. All denominations with which I am familiar, and which have been around for more than a hundred years, have seen the spiritual value of such retreats for the presider. Again, you can't give what you don't have.

As the presider of public worship and public prayer services, the chaplain must be aware of the latest developments in liturgical music, prayer structures (sacramental expressions), and sacramental spiritual theologies. Again, all faith groups and denominations that have been around for more than a hundred years have these structures. Those which have been around for less than a hundred years have such theologies and structures in a nascent form, but have not yet recognized them by the same terminologies, because they are so absorbed, by necessity, in developing their reasons for existence and their roots.

The consequence of all this for the chaplain is the need to attend those workshops her denomination conducts for their clergy in liturgical, musical, and aesthetical theology. Customarily, those workshops are conducted once or twice a year for one day for each presentation. Occasionally, a faith group or denomination will have a more extensive and intensive special meeting regarding these areas of public worship. These meetings occur on a two, three or five year cycle for a period of three to five days. The chaplain must make it her business to attend these workshops. You can't give what you don't have.

Following our analogy of the surgeon, the surgeon must attend workshops and classes every year, conducted by experienced surgeons, to remain abreast of the latest insights and practices within her profession in order that her patients may receive the advantage of the best medical science has to offer. Do the taxpayers expect the chaplains to do anything less for the inmates, who need life-correcting heart surgery? Continuing education must be seen as professional nourishment for the life of a healthy correctional chaplain.

To those who would propose that there are no such developments within the worship structure, sacramental or prayer life of faith communities, the proper response is this: "Those who are unaware of the development of history are doomed to repeat its mistakes and miss its opportunities." I would add that the chaplain, who denies the development of theology, whether it be pastoral, dogmatic, liturgical, biblical or moral, should not be in the chaplaincy in the first place or in ministry at all. To put it another way, the person who denies that two plus two equals four is the person who has heard of mathematics but has never studied or practiced it.

The history of developed public worship and public prayer is older than the written history of mankind. Any well-trained clergy person would know that and see it as self-evident. To deny herself those resources is to consciously deny her role as a responsible minister of her faith group. Her irresponsibility would have a direct effect upon her ministry to the inmates.

For those faith groups not of his own, it is the direct responsibility of the chief provider of the institution, the chaplain, to reach out to the leadership of those faith groups in civilian society to negotiate with them for the services of responsible spiritual leaders, who will conduct public worship and prayer services for the inmates of those faith groups. The chaplain, who will not do that or drags his feet in providing for the inmates, is either lazy or spiritually uncertain of his own faith, finding these groups threatening to his prayer life. In either event, such a person does not belong in chaplaincy. That is, the person of faith must be secure in his own faith journey in order not to be threatened by other faith expressions different from his own.

In order to be the interpreter for the administration about the various religious practices of these other faith groups, it is the responsibility of the chaplain to see that he is present when these other faith groups have their worship and prayer services. It is never appropriate for a chaplain to be regularly absent when another faith group is having their main worship service of the week. If it means that the chaplain has to adjust his schedule in order to live up to this standard, the answer is to be found in the first and primary role of a chaplain. He is a servant.

If the chaplain's schedule becomes an inconvenience to her family, the chaplain should remember that she did not answer the call of ministry to inmates for the convenience of her family any more than she would have answered the call to civilian congregational ministry for the convenience of her family. These very practical problems should be resolved with the assistance of the leadership of her denomination. In every real sense, the clergy person's family shares in her ministry, no matter where it is and to whom she ministers. The family often needs help to recommit itself to make this sacrifice for the sake of clergy person's ministry. If that cannot be done, for ministry within the prison, the chaplain should consider another area of ministry.

There is no other profession that works with state government that requires a family to make such a sacrifice. The chaplain may be at home, but he cannot be with his family because he has to give a talk at a church in the community in an attempt to attract volunteers to assist in the prison ministry. The chaplain may be at home, but he cannot be with his family because he has to spend hours working on his sermon. The chaplain may be at home, but he cannot be with his family while he pursues his theological and spiritual reading. The chaplain may be home, but he cannot be with his family because he is interrupted three or four times a day by phone calls from volunteers rearranging their schedules or planning future worship services. He may be at home, but he cannot be with his family because he has to write the monthly report, or the annual report, or write a response to a legal challenge from an inmate, or write a report for the attorneys in central office. He had planned to do these reports at the office, but that day four inmates had to be notified of deaths or medical emergencies in their families. After those necessary interruptions were finished, there was no time or energy to write the reports. The beat goes on, and the family waits.

The chaplain's family may worship once a week, but not with him. Again, this is a major change from civilian ministry. The chaplain's family may have school celebrations and holiday celebrations, but not with him. Either he is totally absent from family events or he is late for most of them in order to minister to the inmates, who also need a presider at the holidays and other major events in their lives. If the spouse and children are not in harmony with this ministry and the family sacrifices it entails, they frequently leave. The dichotomy between family commitments and institutional ministry is the source of major stress and must be considered when answering the call to the chaplaincy. Parenthetically, it should be noted that one of the first words connected with the priestly role throughout history is sacrifice.

Just as the clergy person in civilian society, the chaplain is often referred to as "preacher." From the prison administrators to the line officers, very few people understand the magnitude of the responsibilities the chaplain must carry, let alone the struggle to find the time to do the research, the meditation and writing for that which he is most commonly known — preaching. No other profession that works with state government has to spend so much uncompensated time to perform the duties for which it is hired.

The chaplain as presider must also give public expression to the role of prayer at times other than the main worship service of the week. Every major faith group teaches that prayer and worship is not something that is done just once a week, but it is a whole and healthy part of everyday life. For this reason, the chaplain must participate in a leadership way in public prayer every day he is in the institution. The institution has far more social workers than chaplains; far more psychologists than chaplains; far more teachers than chaplains; far more health service personnel than chaplains. But it has only one or two leaders of prayer. If the chaplain's denomination does not recommend or require a daily public prayer service, the chaplain can creatively design a devotion service from the prayers his denomination recommends participants practice in their homes.

Regardless of the format, the chaplain must give public witness on a daily basis to the fact that prayer and worship are an integral part of a healthy, stable, mature and fruitful adult life — the kind of life we expect from the inmate when he is released to society.

The chaplain must make it known to the prison administrators that a daily time of prayer is as important as the main worship service of the week. As a consequence, the chaplain will not cancel daily devotions or worship in order to attend staff meetings or write reports that are requested by the central office or for any other function. To do so would contradict the essential role for which he was hired — to serve the inmates, not the staff.

Besides, no conscientious administrator would schedule staff meetings when the inmates are most available to his staff. That would be an act in contradiction of the nature of the role of the administrator as a rehabilitator and public servant. Body language is ninety percent of all communication. How we *act* reinforces what we *say* as administrators and clergy. The chaplain as presider at worship must uphold this standard at all times.

There is absolutely nothing more important to his role as a chaplain than being the presider at prayer and public worship. Except for this primary function, nearly every other part of his role as a clergy person can be performed in some modified way by non-ordained persons. For this reason, a good chaplain must know when to delegate.

Originator:

The chaplain is in charge of, and responsible for, all worship and prayer services that occur within the institution. This means that she sets the schedule, length and frequency of the services to be provided. It is never the role of the warden or deputy warden to make these decisions. Obviously, the chaplain must recognize the limitations that are naturally imposed by the need of the inmates to be in their locked quarters for count at various times of the day. It would be a most rare event for which the chaplain would ask the warden and deputy wardens to alter the schedule of the institution to accommodate a worship service.

Most institutions have the inmates available to the chaplain and her programs for three sessions of two to two and a half hour periods per day. That is adequate for nearly every faith group's routine services. At times of high holy days or the visitation of special spiritual guests, the chaplain should consult with the warden and deputy wardens a month in advance to arrange with all department heads involved in any changes in schedule, or special facilities, equipment or supplies that may be needed. At no time will a chaplain permit any program of any faith group to run beyond its allotted time, whether for routine or special services. Special services may be for such occasions as Ramadan, Christmas, Easter, Hanukkah, retreats, revivals, cantatas and the visit of a faith groups judicatory. Every major faith group has such observances and pastoral visitations. It is the chaplain who is responsible for knowing what is spiritually and legally best within a prison setting for the proper observance of these occasions.

To follow our analogy one more step, a lawyer does not tell a surgeon how to perform an appendectomy or when to perform it. If the lawyer has some question about the professional judgment and skills of the surgeon, it is incumbent upon the lawyer to consult a medical board of review. In the prison setting, if the warden or deputy wardens have a question about the time needed for a faith group's worship services and believes that the chaplain did not give completely accurate or adequate information, it is incumbent upon the warden or deputy wardens to consult the chief chaplains in central office.

It is always inappropriate for a warden or deputy warden to presume to tell the chaplain how long to preach or pray. While such interference is probably illegal and certainly unethical, at the very least it is a mark of ignorance and grossly impolite.

When an inmate complains about or questions the appropriateness of the religious services offered in the prison, the warden or deputy warden should immediately direct all such issues to the chaplain. In turn, the chaplain has a duty to keep the warden and deputy warden informed of her response to the inmate. Professional and courteous communication is the hallmark in all such issues for both the warden, the deputy wardens and the chaplains.

Of all worship and prayer services:

There is no faith group that is foreign to a chaplain. It is his role to see to it that the beliefs and practices of all faith groups are protected as long as those practices are not contrary to obvious common sense security rules.

At no time may the administration set up or establish a faith group. Nor may they manage a faith group's program outside the chaplain's jurisdiction. For example, the administration may do nothing to establish Bible study groups or other prayer or faith group activities in the dormitories or cell blocks beyond what the chaplain has provided. Neither may the administration ever bring in or authorize persons other than chaplains to conduct or lead or supervise such services without the authority of the chaplain being respected and permission and supervision being given and provided.

If anybody in the administration believes the chaplain's programs are inadequate for the inmates' needs, it is the responsibility of that person to consult with the chaplain and to follow the chaplain's directions in these matters. If there is a point of questioning the judgment of the chaplain, the chief chaplain in central office should be consulted and his decision followed.

To continue the analogy of the surgeon, a person who has read an article in *The New England Journal of Medicine* would not presume, on that basis, that the people in an institution that she manages are not receiving enough surgery or the right kind of surgery. She certainly would not, on the basis of the article alone, go out and hire another surgeon to perform more surgery. In the same vein, a warden or deputy warden, just because they might be an active member of a faith group, should not presume to have the pastoral training and experience of the chaplain. While reading the article in the magazine may cause the warden or deputy warden to talk to the surgeon about new procedures in the science of medicine, so would she consult with the chaplain if her understanding of faith practices seems to differ from what she sees happening in the religious services department of her institution.

Finally, if the chaplain is called upon to provide an invocation or benediction for inmate or staff functions, the chaplain's services should be provided with the following in mind. Is the chaplain being invited because there is a link with religion and the inmate or staff function, or is the chaplain being invited because, "It is the thing to do"? It is a customary "thing to do" to hang ornaments on a pine tree at Christmas or to place a United States flag on a stage. If there is truly a spiritual dimension to the purpose of the meeting or ceremony, then by all means the chaplain belongs there. Unfortunately, our present American culture has grown into a very bad habit of inviting "The Reverend" because it seems "the thing to do." The chaplain, who responds to those sorts of invitations with her presence is continuing the insult to all religions.

Religion is not a perfunctory part of life. It is an essential and equally-important part of life as is physical nourishment and health. It is as important and essential as mental health and education. If a chaplain participates at those times when he is being used as the "expected" piece of decoration on the printed program or on the stage, his body language may speak a lie to the value of religion in a rehabilitated, mature and responsible life.

On the other hand, if there is a religious value to the group's meeting, those who invite the chaplain for an invocation or benediction should allow the chaplain sufficient time to pray in accordance with the purpose of the meeting. Customarily, that would be about five minutes. Also, it is the responsibility of the chaplain not to abuse the time offered him by running on ad nauseam with a superfluity of prayer, in effect attempting to be the uninvited featured speaker. Common sense and courtesy should be extended both ways. The final judgment call on whether or not to attend such meetings, ceremonies or celebrations is always the chaplain's. The administration is always out of place to pressure the chaplain to attend.

Finally, it needs to be said that the image of General George Patton, in the movie "Patton," telling his chaplain what and how to pray, is a Hollywood caricature that needs to be put asunder. As a hospital administrator would not presume to tell a heart surgeon what is the proper technique for performing heart surgery, so is it just as ludicrous and insulting for a prison administrator to presume to tell the chaplain what to pray, how to pray and how long to pray. Unfortunately, I had such a supervisor once. He insisted that the grave side service for a deceased inmate not exceed five minutes in length. There were no weather conditions or other circumstances necessitating or justifying such a cursory show of ceremony. It just so happened that the administrator had a gross dislike, or should we say fear, of death. I suggested he not attend the ceremony. He did anyway, but did not interrupt the ceremony as he had threatened.

CHAPTER THREE

THE CHAPLAIN AS TEACHER

The chaplain *leads the inmates and staff to a deeper understanding of the religious principles they profess in their hearts.* The heart surgeon performs the penultimate skills of his profession in the surgical suite. In today's Information Age, the surgeon must also possess communication skills to relate to non-surgeons what and why he does what he does, lest they begin to think they know how to operate on themselves. The chaplain's role as teacher is somewhat similar. There are many teachers in the institution. However, there are none who are as skilled in the delicate ways, practices, history and profession of so many deeply-held beliefs in a Power beyond any that can be fathomed with the knowledge and experience of this world as he. It is appropriate to see the chaplain as the resident theologian, who should be consulted on all theological matters.

Leads:

The word "educator" comes from a Latin root that means "one who leads another out" — to lead one out of the darkness of ignorance into the light of truth. But a leader, who does not know where she has been, where she is, or where she is going, is no better off than those she pretends to lead. In fact, she may be doing them more harm than good. For, by her words, they may believe they know more than they really do. Then they may fall into greater harm to themselves as a result of their inculpable ignorance. For example, you may lead a person to believe that the highway she is on leads to a beautiful beach, where she will find rest and relaxation. But the truth is you are not skilled in reading a map and have directed the person down an unmarked road that leads to a cliff and almost certain death.

A chaplain, who professes to teach about the knowledge of God, while he doesn't know the teachings and insights of religious leaders before him, may very well lead his people into destructive fanaticism. This sort of ignorance has led to the loss of hundreds of millions of lives in the name of God.

The chaplain as teacher does not doubt the sincerity of the faith of inmates and staff. However, she must know that a person does not live by bread alone, neither does a person live by faith alone. In her own life, she must know that her beliefs are related to all the other actions of her daily life.

As teacher and leader, the chaplain is working with many other people throughout the day, who are highly-skilled in various fields of learning and research. All of these fields are bodies of knowledge about a certain aspect of truth. The chaplain knows that all truth is interrelated. From his perspective, the truth of God is the glue that holds all the other schools of knowledge together.

In our age, information is readily available in libraries, the press, visual media, and through computers. Masses of people can know a little about a lot of things. They can sometimes be falsely led to believe they know a lot about a lot of things. The same is true with religious beliefs. Media commentators often come across as authorities when they have actually missed the vital subtleties of the truth of a matter.

Thus, the first role of the chaplain as teacher is to get her head on straight. She must push her God-given brain to its limits. She must search the depths of the teachings of her denomination. She must comprehend the nuances of its teachings. She must be in tune with its teachers and leaders as they search for the latest insights into the truths about God and where that leads civilization in this age.

But knowledge of theological dogmas and insights into sacred writings is not enough, The chaplain is also looked to as a leader in the broader fields of knowledge that affect the lives of the inmates and staff. He must understand many of the philosophies current in this age. He must be able to communicate clearly about the world of ideas that lead people and governments and societies to behave and structure themselves the way they do. He must have a knowledge of the workings of government and the basic principles of law that guide the agencies of secular authority.

She must have a profound understanding of and also a respect for foreign languages. She must understand how easily the nuances of the meanings of words can cause wars, delay the writings of peace treaties, fuel schisms and challenge councils. She must have a basic knowledge of the empirical sciences. She must know how to distinguish the real pioneering research of gifted scientists from that of quacks, who pretend they are gifted. She must clearly have a deep appreciation for the talent of a theologian, whose knowledge has been made available for the service of the church. At the same time, she must not be afraid to speak of the emptiness of the flashy television preachers/entertainers.

She must have an experience of, and appreciation for, the arts — music, poetry, painting, sculpture and architecture. She must have an understanding of, and an appreciation for how these bodies of knowledge and experience can lift the mind and heart to truths above and beyond this world. She must understand and appreciate how these bodies of knowledge can lead us to a more peaceful and harmonious life.

The chaplain should have a basic knowledge of the science of nature, and the physical and psychological science of humankind. He must have a deep appreciation for the great gift of nature and its delicate balance that has been given to us by God to be used by people in a way that conserves that balance. He must be able to speak to physicians and psychologists in a way that he and they can understand so that his parishioners are served in the best possible way. The chaplain must understand how his body of knowledge can compliment the body of truth out of which the physician and the psychologist are working or using as a point of reference.

The chaplain must also have a knowledge and love of history. There is an old saying that the person who does not know history is doomed to repeat its mistakes. It is also said that the person who does not know history will miss its opportunities. The chaplain must know where her body of truth fits in. She must know the mistakes her predecessors have made. She must know the insights that can be repeated validly today. There is no need to reinvent the wheel with each new generation.

With all of the above, it is highly recommended that a chaplain have a broad base of knowledge and a degree in the humanities, with at least a minor in philosophy.

When it comes to theological truths and insights, the chaplain must have a detailed knowledge of the teachings of his own denomination. He must know what it professes, why it professes, how it professes, and to whom it professes its beliefs. He must have a firm grasp of its religious history, the development of its creed, and the latest scholarly insights about its revealed truths. He must clearly know its moral teachings, its philosophy of life, its teachings about faith and science and its perspective on the use of the arts. He should know from deep within his heart its form of public worship, and its principles of private prayer and meditation. He must know what his denomination's views are on secular authority, the structure of its schools and administration, and its public relationship with other religions.

As a minimum, it is inconceivable that a chaplain can amass this body of knowledge with anything less than a Masters of Divinity degree obtained from nothing less than an accredited theological school. Such a program should be at least a three year curriculum. A five year program would be preferred. This would include a year of internship at a congregational setting of his denomination.

Some may argue that it does not take this long to come to the experience of faith. That is true. But it takes at least this much knowledge for the chaplain to know what she doesn't know. It is this humility that is the seed and seat of all wisdom. She absolutely must know where her body of truth fits in with the rest of the people with whom and to whom she will be ministering. There is only one thing worse than a pompous cleric, and that is the pompous cleric who makes a fool of God rather than trying to be a fool for God.

It is an absolutely essential thing for the chaplain to know first and foremost *whose* she is. In that perspective, she will begin to know *who* she is. There is no knowledge of whose we are without being grounded deeply in humility. Being clearly grounded deeply in her being as a humble servant of God will be the anchor that gets the chaplain through the storms of state bureaucracy, when she is treated as a humiliated slave.

Finally, the chaplain is working in a secular setting with people, who are suffering severe inabilities to cope with the normal challenges of our modern life. The chaplain will be one among a number of professionals, who will be working with the inmate to restore him to a wholeness of life where he can leave the institutional setting to live a full and productive life. To be able to communicate those values and goals and to work with others who have similar goals, the chaplain should have at least six months of special training in a clinical setting where he can get to know his own personal weaknesses, while at the same time learning to communicate honestly with other professionals and the inmates with whom they will be working. Through this training, he will learn how and when to seek and accept referrals from other professionals.

Throughout all this she must be deepening her skills as a listener — a listener to her own feelings, and a listener to the feelings of others. To the degree she can improve that skill, she may be able to listen more deeply to the God in whom she professes belief.

In short, once again, you can't give what you don't have. You can't teach what you don't know. You can't lead, if you don't know where you have come from, where you are, and where you plan to go.

The inmates and staff:

The religious experiences of inmates and staff are at about the same level. Some have continued to attend their faith groups from youth through adolescence and into adulthood, growing in knowledge and experience along the way. Unfortunately, though, most inmates and staff stopped having an active community experience of God at about the fourth or fifth grade. Thus, while they are in adult bodies and have adult minds, they tend to relate to God and those who minister in God's name from the perspective of children. So very often that perspective is one of fear, rather than reverence. The unspoken message of their body language is often acted out in this manner: "If I am not good in the presence of this minister, God will get me." So the chaplain often hears adult men and women, inmates and staff, cursing and swearing, shouting and hollering at one another until he comes around the corner. Then, those same "adult" people act like little children, who have just been caught with their hands in the cookie jar. They offer profuse and childlike apologies.

It is a challenge for the chaplain to lead these people to an adult understanding of a loving creator. They need to hear from the chaplain that God is compassionate, while at the same time the chaplain must lead them to an adult realization that God is no fool. It is a challenge for the chaplain to teach convincingly both the inmates and the staff that God is merciful. On top of all this, he must communicate that God created mind and body and emotions, and that God made all these parts of the human being very good. Finally, the chaplain must rise to the challenge of communicating to the inmates and the staff that God communicates to us all in an adult way through written and personal inspiration.

In the secular arena, a teacher follows a lesson plan, a plan for the day that fits into the plan for the year. Each daily plan is designed to lead the student from what she has already been taught and understood to new levels of knowledge, to an ever expanding base and depth. The chaplain as teacher has to work upon much the same plane. Her "students" have some knowledge. However, in most cases the students have no idea what they don't know. What is worse is that very many of them do not want to learn at all. Such inmates and staff approach God from the simple notion that God is unchanging and, therefore, a fifth grader's knowledge of God and His ways is unchanging and adequate. A large number of these people with this mindset are easily threatened by any serious efforts at attempting to expand the mind's understanding of God's ways in an adult world.

Thus, the chaplain has to be both a leader and a cheerleader, both pulling and shoving. He has to be encouraging and frequently challenging his people to an ever richer adult understanding of God. At the same time, he has to be ever so careful not to get too far ahead of his students. At all times he must be able to help them relate their growing knowledge to their growing experience.

For the vast majority of inmates their experience of worshipping God in a public, community setting has included loud music, highly-emotional preaching and occasional dancing. The whole worship environment was designed to appeal to the senses. It was not designed to appeal to sense. The chaplain as teacher must be willing to show that the two can go hand in glove. All that can be truly human can be truly sacred. Thus, while making a joyful noise unto the Lord is good and holy, using the brain to sort out medical ethics and morals is also good and holy.

As a teacher, the chaplain needs to be able to show that a child's Bible study program is comparable to a child's mathematics study program. From that base, she then need to be able to teach that an adult study program does not do away with what the adult learned as a child, but builds on that knowledge as multiplication builds on addition. The chaplain as teacher must show that adult Bible studies lead to revealing God as far more marvelously and richly involved in our lives than we have been able to understand as children. It is the chaplain's challenge to present the sacred writings to the inmates for each of their faith groups in such a way that they come to understand how adults of their faith groups have lived and interpreted these writings in an adult manner over many centuries.

Since we live in a visual age, in an age of visual media, it is the responsibility of the chaplain to present religious education through the latest electronic media and technology. Because eighty percent of the inmates have stunted reading abilities, the chaplain must use video movies, audio cassettes, slide projectors, and overhead projectors. He must also search for volunteer group leaders that are skilled in these audio and visual media, with the abilities to present truth and facts in a dynamic manner. Entertainment is not the goal; education is. While that is true, we still must start at the level where we find our students and make use of the means of communications that our society is used to. The chaplain must build on what his students know and lead them to where their faith group says adult members of their group should be.

To face the challenge of a secular, materialistic age that is by and large devoid of moral and sacred teachings, it is absolutely necessary for the chaplain to give equal emphasis, hour for hour, to religious education as she does to public worship. If two hours are provided for worship, two hours of religious education should be provided for each faith group. This is not a luxury. This is an absolute necessity, if we are to prepare the minds of the inmates for the fight against secular ideas, philosophies and habits that brought them to prison in the first place. Singing and dancing and loud preaching will never be enough. They will always leave the inmates half empty and, therefore, half-prepared to lead a spiritually-healthy and balanced life.

Because the chaplain is usually a respected person by the inmates, it is also absolutely necessary for the chaplain to encourage the inmates to develop their minds in the arena of secular education. He should urge them all to finish their high school education. Knowing that the lack of education will keep people perennially unemployed in civilian society, he must use his influence to urge them to develop all the skills and talents God gave them. When they have finished their G.E.D.s, he should urge and encourage them to go on to technical and college level studies as they are available and as far as their talents will take them inside the prison and after their confinement. If he believes that all of life is a gift from God, to be returned to God as fully developed as possible, the chaplain can do nothing less than lead the inmates through the various levels of secular and religious education as well.

A few years ago an inmate asked to work as a porter at the Religious Services Center. I told him I wouldn't hire him unless he went to school to finish his G.E.D. After he graduated with his G.E.D., he came to say that he was ready to go to work. I told him to get out a piece of paper, to date it, and to write on it that the chaplain lied to him. I told him he couldn't work for us because he had achieved the highest grade of anybody in our institution on his G.E.D. test. I told him I would be committing a sin, if I let him work for us and he did not get a chance to expand his mind through one of our vocational or technical programs. He enrolled in our computer-assisted design program and was paroled the next year. While using those skills to get an eighteen dollar an hour job, he enrolled in a private college to take evening courses. He will graduate in three years. In recent years, three other inmates from our faith group have also gone on to continue their education after parole. I have heard from their pastors that all of them have also stayed active with the church after parole.

It is our practice at our institution to encourage the inmates to develop and expand their knowledge in things secular and sacred. Over the last ten years, eighty-two percent of those who have completed the G.E.D. program or graduated with an associate's degree, when those programs were offered, have been active participants in one of our eight faith groups. At any given time, nearly forty percent of our active faith group members are in school.

Just as the chaplain does not have time to devote long-term energies to counseling civilian employees, acting as one who refers staff to civilian pastors, so too, in matters of education, the chaplain can be a source of encouragement to staff members who have not completed their high school education, and to those who could benefit from continuing education programs or college degrees.

Within the field of continuing education, at the very least the chaplain should have a two-hour program available per year for the training officers, to be used in their programs for the training of all employees. Those areas in which staff members may run into problems about religious issues should be updated and featured each year. The correctional officers, the nurses, the social workers, the teachers, the cooks — all need to know what is acceptable behavior and what is not for the faith groups that are active in the institution.

They need to be constantly reminded to call the chaplains, whenever an issue of a religious nature comes up. The staff needs to be reassured the chaplain will give them, or get for them the correct answer and guidance. The employers need to be reminded that an improper response to a religious issue may result in a federal lawsuit and can result in the loss of life, if they are not careful.

To a deeper understanding of the religious principles they profess in their hearts:

When teaching high school in the 1960's, I used to do a lot of role playing to get the lessons across to the students. In one class, in an attempt to teach the evils of racial bias, I pretended to be Governor George Wallace. The students were supposed to tell me why my positions about race were wrong. At one point, one of the students became so frustrated when she failed to counter my positions that she started to cry. She knew in her heart what was right and what was wrong, but she could not articulate it. At that time she could not defend her position, as correct as it was.

It is the challenge of the chaplain to give his inmates the substance of truth on which to anchor their feelings. When they go back to their dorms or cells or to their homes in the civilian community, people will ask them or challenge them about their beliefs. They must be able to say more than, "Because I believe it is so." They must be given the tools to know how to think about things religious and the tools to express those sacred values and teachings.

As alluded to above, the chaplain's role is not to tear down what has been learned as a child, but to build on it. He is never to ridicule the past, but to give a solid vision for the present and the future. What he teaches must be in harmony with the Author of All Truth, so that those truths will resonate in the hearts of those being led to the Author.

One day, while I was sitting on a hillside in southern Ohio, away from all the sounds of civilization on a spring afternoon, I put a cassette tape in the portable player to listen to music by Mozart. After a few minutes of listening to the music, I noticed the robins in the field in front of me. They were hopping from spot to spot in search of worms. Then it occurred to me that the music and the robins were moving in harmony to the same rhythm. I said to myself, "Good old Mozart. He was no dummy. He tried to capture in sound the beauty of the rhythm of nature." Those sounds have lifted the minds and hearts of millions of people for the last two hundred years to the glory and majesty of the Author of All Sound.

That is the role of the chaplain as teacher, to coordinate and orchestrate all that is known about the truths of God to such a pitch in each person's heart that they, with solid knowledge and poetry-filled hearts, may give full glory to God. It is that orchestrated harmony of mind and heart and soul that the chaplain hopes the inmate will live out in a life of love of God and neighbor, until he is called to be at home forever with the Author of All Love, All Truth, and All Beauty.

CHAPTER FOUR

THE CHAPLAIN AS MEDIATOR

"You have 2,500 inmates who don't want to be here. You have 500 workers, many of whom are tired of being sworn at and ordered around as if they were inmates; others of whom don't want to work Saturday and Sunday and third shift to boot! And you ask if there is tension in our prison?!" Thus answered a correctional officer to a civilian volunteer. The word "mediate" comes from the Latin word "mediatus." Its original meaning was "to be in the middle." The first dictionary meaning is "to interpose between parties in order to reconcile them." The mediator is one who is an agent between parties at variance.

Most people would not think of a surgeon as a mediator. Yet there are a number of potential and real conflicts he has to mediate before he enters the surgical suite, and while he is in the surgical suite; sometimes even after the surgery. Most patients, if they had a real choice, would not want to undergo surgery. The operating room staff has to be carefully chosen. The surgeon not only has to be certain of their supporting skills, but must make sure that they work in harmony, regardless of personality differences. In these days, before entering the surgical suite, the surgeon has to make his case convincingly to a finance officer representing the board of directors, that the surgical pro-

41

cedure is justifiable at this time, at this cost, and that liability insurance is sufficient to defend against potential lawsuits. The surgeon also has to be a skilled communicator in explaining to the patient and her family the results of the surgery, and any complications rising therefrom. Especially must he be skilled as a communicator, if the patient dies. Finally, the surgeon has to have his actions and procedures reviewed by and found justifiable by the college of surgeons. All of these potential and real conflicts and differences the surgeon has to deal with in the name of preserving and restoring health.

A chaplain, as a spiritual healer, has many of the same potential and real differences to reconcile and negotiate among similar groups in the name of being able to pray. Very often the inmates, who need her help, don't want it and prefer to treat their spiritual ills with self-diagnosis. With high divorce rates, undeveloped spiritual lives, and an ethical system based upon retribution, a sizeable portion of correctional staff also stand in need of inner healing, before the mission of the prison can be effective. Next, the chaplain has to deal with following orders from some central office staff, who have been removed from day to day workings with inmates for so long that they have forgotten what spiritual healing is like. These folks often seem more concerned with avoiding potential lawsuits and "dumbing down" religious practices to a commonality that would make gruel appealing. The inmates' families also have concerns and worries and angers and moments of grief to be worked through. Then there are the churches, masjids, temples and synagogues that do not all speak with one voice within their denominations, when they have expectations of what religious practices should be observed within the institution. Inmate to inmate spiritual conflicts also cause the chaplain to be a mediator. Finally, contrary to the non-scholarly bias of some faith groups, the chaplain is the mediator between the inmate and God.

Not all these conflicts and differences can be clearly defined and delineated. Often the resolution to a difference will involve players from several groups listed above. At those times, the chaplain feels like she is refereeing a football game, a soccer game, a hockey game and a basketball game on the same court at the same time. There some days when the wisdom of Solomon and the patience of Job seem to pale in comparison to what the chaplain feels she is called upon to do. At least Solomon only had to offer the women two choices — cut the baby in half or give it intact to one of the two parties. Many days the chaplain feels her choices are being made in the midst of a furious triage. When she goes home at night she hopes she cut the baby into the right pieces. She had no choice to keep it whole.

Many inmates have the mistaken notion that the chaplain has all the answers to their problems. On top of that, they believe that the answers they want to their problems are the right answers, and that the chaplain should be a creative magician and provide the solution the inmate wants. Trying to mediate the differences between their desires and expectations and what is really going to happen or permitted to happen, can result in outbursts of anger or long-lasting and silent rejection. Occasionally an inmate will get up after being told the solution he wants is not workable, and on the way out of the office looks back and says, "I thought you would help me." At those times, the chaplain would like to say to the inmate, "I did help you, and you didn't recognize it." He refrains from vocalizing the response, knowing the inmate would see it as a sarcastic and flippant rejection of what he felt was a real problem.

In civilian society, when the surgeon's patient is not satisfied that she received proper care, she will tell her family and friends. The surgeon may lose potential future patients. In the prison, when an inmate doesn't get the solution he's looking for from the chaplain, he will go back to his dorm or unit and vociferously put down the chaplain. He may even stand in front of the Religious Services Center and tell other inmates not to go in. Of course, his last act of revenge is to stop going to his faith group meetings. The inmate's unacknowledged logic is something like this: "You deprived me, so I'm going to deprive myself."

While there are many supportive civilian staff members, the chaplain will find himself caught in the cross hairs of anger from a civilian who has had a falling out with members or clergy of her church back home. In their minds, the chaplain represents all people related to some faith group, so the civilian can wind up living out her anger by frustrating the cooperation the chaplain needs to work effectively with the inmates.

I once heard of an employee, who had an argument with his pastor and left the church of his birth. Next, the employee's wife ran off with an inmate. Then the employee came to work in the business office of a prison. You can imagine the cooperation the chaplain received when he needed to order supplies and materials for the faith groups of that prison. It took two years before the chaplain could find an avenue of communication that helped the employee work through his pain. At that point, the requests for purchases were approved in record time.

The chaplain as mediator has to be patient with inmates and civilians alike, giving them time and space to work through their immediate angers and pains and to see the chaplain as a person, who is there to help with the healing process, not to be an agent of rejection and punishment.

Since the prison is built on a military model, it can become a habit for administrators to relate to civilians, including the chaplain, as automatons with no rights, no feelings, and no brains. As parents sometimes get frustrated with the behavior of their children and will take the easy way out by punishing all the children for what one did wrong, so administrators, locally and at central office, can fall into the trap in a prison of making blanket solutions to what was an individual or isolated problem. As a parent gets overwhelmed and tired, so do administrative staff. Their actions and decisions affect all — inmates, staff and chaplains.

In the middle of this, the chaplain, as one who feels he has been equally wronged by a blanket and thoughtless and unfeeling decision, must nonetheless rise above the moment. She must attempt to talk to the administrators behind closed doors and at a quiet time, to give the administrators a chance to see the effect of what they have done, to save face, to work through their frustrations and to make corrections. When the chaplain is dealing with a person who has a weak ego, the chaplain's job can seem to be nearly insurmountable.

On a small scale, I can recall the day a warden issued an order that, effective immediately, only Totes umbrellas would be allowed in the institution. It was raining heavily that day. It was two days before pay day. There was no advance notice given for the order. Fortunately, I was able to catch the warden in a quiet and private moment. I told him of the emotional reaction among the employees, and the impact his order was having on morale. Many employees did not have the money to buy new umbrellas, and no one had the time. All were getting wet. After expressing his valid concern for the security threat that large umbrellas posed inside the fence, the warden rescinded his order and re-issued a new one that would be effective a week later.

On another occasion, with four hours to go before the start

of the month-long observance of fast by Muslims, Ramadan, we were notified by central office that we had to change how, when and where we served the daily meals. Also, food items were changed on the menu. What we had been doing locally for ten years had been working well. With a flurry of phone calls, and a change of orders three times in that four hour period, it was finally resolved to do what we had been doing all along and begin the new procedures the next year.

There has been a long history of custom built up in the civilian community to call a chaplain, whether in the military or in a hospital or in a prison, when a family member has a crisis. It is also a long custom that the family members believe that a chaplain is available seven days a week and all day long. As our voice mail indicates, it is not unusual for a family member to call at ten or eleven at night and all day Saturday and Sunday. While many of these calls are about illnesses or deaths in the inmate's family, other times they call about problems in the visiting room, the mail room, the prison hospital, or perceived threats on the life of the inmate. Frequently, these family members and friends are in an excited state.

Often, when there is a death in the inmate's family, the family member will insist on being the one to tell the inmate the bad news. It must be explained to them that it is healthier for the inmate, and keeps the chaplain from being forced to play into some form of deception, when the chaplain informs the inmate for the family. Family members usually calm down enough to understand why it is best for the chaplain to break the news, and then to put the inmate in touch with the family as soon as is practical.

When family members have problems with other departments in the institution, it is most often because they just do not understand the reasons for the rules and policies. By patient listening and careful explanation, the chaplain can most often get the family members calmed down and direct them to an amiable solution to their problem. Frequently, the family members just did not know what department and what person to speak to. From time to time, I have received thank you notes from family members, who were irate when they first called but were able to get help after our conversation. Again, as mediator, the chaplain has to listen carefully and be well-informed about the resources of the institution.

"Chaplain, God has laid it on my heart that I have to come into your institution this Sunday to preach so that souls will not go to hell." Every chaplain, who has been around for a while, has had this kind of phone call from the self-appointed, self-anointed "ministers of God." After rejecting the impulse to thank the caller for implying that the chaplain is not doing his job, the chaplain has to patiently explain to the ignorant the policies and procedures that the prison has to follow before permitting outside resources to assist with ministry to the inmates. When some understand that they will not be getting into the institution on a moment's notice, they will write the governor or central office or the warden to complain. By the same token, many are never heard from again. The chaplain as mediator has to show these people the same respect and courtesy as though they were talking to the leader of their own denomination.

"You have the wrong group of people coming into your institution to minister to the members of our faith group. They do not represent the real teachings of our faith. They are not credentialed. They don't follow the right books of interpretation of our faith." Again, the chaplain gets calls from these representatives of faith groups, who feel they have the Truth, and the group that the chaplain uses does not. Almost all faith groups have factions. Some are more splintered than others. With the limits of space and time, the chaplain cannot satisfy all factions. As a mediator she tries to look for a consensus among the main factions within a faith group to determine if there is enough of a common ground that most of the essential teachings of the group can be observed under the security regulations of the prison. So very often it happens that a consensus cannot be reached, and so the chaplain has to make a decision to work with that faction that seems to be the most mature in their demeanor and presentation of services. At all times, the chaplain is aware that there will be tension among the men, among the civilian leaders of the faith group, and that a lawsuit is a real possibility. Parenthetically, it has been my experience that when a non-chaplain prison administrator attempts to step in to settle a conflict over a religious matter, the conflicting parties wind up increasing their venom and anger. As long as there are these factions within major faith groups, the chaplain will have to be willing to be a mediator, often times being taken for "the bad guy."

Even when a group is permitted to come to the Religious Services Center to minister to a particular faith group, the services do not always work out well. Even though the leaders of the volunteer group have been told not to preach against another religion, some will do so in defiance, saying that "God told them to do so." They will not accept the chaplain telling them that God is not a God of disorder and disrespect. As a mediator, the chaplain has to tell these groups that they are no longer welcome to inflict their confusion upon a captive audience. Through it all, the chaplain must remain respectful, yet firm and clear in upholding the basis for good order.

"Chaplain, Joe and John are 'girlfriends,' and Joe is singing in your choir. I'm not going to church anymore, until you get Joe out of there." The chaplain as a mediator is called upon to settle religious and moral conflicts between inmates. While our society labels women as being susceptible to spreading gossip, men in prison have cornered the market, when it comes to vicious rumors. Seldom do they actually witness the immoral behavior or directly hear the false teaching that gets them riled up. At the same time, when confronted with their failure to have first-hand evidence of what they believe to be wrong, they will seldom back down and give the other inmate the benefit of the doubt that he might have been falsely accused. Of course, it goes without saying that the inmates follow the civilian fallacy of believing a man is guilty just because he goes to the rules infraction board for a hearing. Many times I have found that the man who went before the board was found innocent, but nobody outside the board room will believe it.

There is an old saying that a mind changed against its will is a mind unchanged still. The chaplain as mediator has the daunting task of getting the conflicting parties to open their minds to the truth, without feeling humiliated in the process. Some people have so little ego strength, that they cannot sustain the change they would have to make in order to accept the truth. They will prefer, instead, the comfort of their anger and rash judgment. To lead some people to accept that the pain of change is less than the pain they are now in is a gift the chaplain as mediator prays for frequently.

Next, there is the role of the mediator between God and man. While one segment of one faith group says there is no such a thing, even though the whole context of their sacred writings says there is, the chaplain is definitely seen by many staff people and most inmates as a conduit to God. "Talk to the chaplain, and he'll pray to God for you and all will be okay." That is the thought process behind many of the requests a chaplain gets for prayer from civilians and inmates alike. I tell the people I work with and serve that I am in sales, not management.

On the other hand, it has been shown that personal and group prayer can be helpful to those who have been inflicted with physical and mental pain. While prayer may be seen by some as a magic potion to the solution of pain and confusion, it has been proven to help a person cope. As I tell the inmates, the garbage dump you are in may not disappear, but your ability to live through it will change measurably, if you become a person of private prayer and a person who shares prayer in community worship. Teaching a person how to pray, and praying with that person to God, is a common role for the chaplain as mediator.

Finally, if the chaplain has been seen to be an effective mediator for inmates and civilians alike, he can make a sizeable contribution to all as a mediator in times of crisis within the institution. There have been numerous cases where chaplains have been involved as hostage negotiators, as mediators to resolve inmate sit-down strikes and riots. During the 1970's, I chaired a negotiating committee of inmates and staff that resolved a sit-down strike. In lesser events, I have helped negotiate the resolution to personal hunger strikes, to threatened suicides, and to men who had refused necessary medical treatment.

Conflict is an unwanted but real ingredient in everyone's life, sooner or later. After working on her own internal and external conflicts in her life during training, a well-skilled chaplain will not necessarily become famous as a mediator. In fact, the better a mediator she is, the less she will be noticed. But the institution will find this part of her pastoral ministry an invaluable tool to the positive growth and security of all who live and work in the prison.

CHAPTER FIVE

THE CHAPLAIN AS ECUMENICAL RECONCILER

The United States is not a pure democracy. While the rule of one man, one vote prevails, each voter is not directly involved in each and every legal decision. We are a republican form of government with elected representatives, who govern our society through the rule of civil law. If our elected representatives do not reflect the combined wisdom of the people, they can be voted out of office. The most fundamental rule of law that our representatives swear to uphold is the Constitution of the United States.

Two hundred years of interpreting that document have highlighted some basic principles. One of the basic principles is the rule of the majority, while at the same time the majority does not rule absolutely. Individual rights are extended to individuals. Individual responsibilities are expected from individuals. Thus, when an American says, "I have my rights," the answer is usually, "Yes you do and no, you don't."

For example, while we have the freedom of speech, we do not have an absolute right to shout "fire" in a crowded theater, when there is no fire. By the same principle, while we have the right to believe the tenets of our religion, we do not have an absolute right to proclaim those teachings in all places and in all circumstances. For example, a community may have a law banning the use of all sound trucks on its streets. By the breadth of that very law, it follows that all churches are then banned from proclaiming their messages by means of sound trucks in that community.

The chaplain in a prison setting is a woman of faith representing to the inmates far more than her personal faith. She carries out her role in a setting that has limitations that are based in the law of the United States. In addition to that law, she must know and follow the basic decencies and courtesies expressed in every major faith. The chaplain is much more than the good humor sort of person who doles out a coordinated schedule of spiritual "Popsicles" full of pious pap for a variety of faith groups to observe their major feasts and holy days.

Since the chaplain carries out the role of pastor in a varied setting that is run in a military fashion by the secular government, it is incumbent upon her to have had some training in constitutional law. She must have a clear legal understanding of just what the separation of church and state means. She must deeply and thoroughly understand that her position in the prison can in no way be used for the furtherance of her faith group's teachings over those of the other faith groups.

There was a case several years ago, where a certain chaplain continually claimed that his prison population of 1850 inmates contained only six Catholics. At the same time, the other prisons in Ohio averaged a Catholic population of ten to twelve percent. He made no effort to substantiate his claim. He provided Catholic services at inconvenient times, at alternate places week by week, and with minimal frequency. The Catholic men wanted to go to church, but they did not know when or where the services were going to be held. Obviously few inmates participated.

At the same time, this chaplain vigorously promoted numerous programs at convenient times for his faith group. The man was fortunate that he was not sued for blatant bias and prejudice. He was not a reconciler. He was a restrictionist. He was a violator of religious freedoms.

Twenty-seven years ago this type of pastoral prejudice and arrogance was common. At a chaplains' meeting in 1970, I sat with three other chaplains for lunch. The three were not of my faith background. They did not speak to me during the entire meal. Over the next several years, each one came to the point where he could apologize for his behavior and laugh at the pathetic ignorance of those times.

The chaplain as ecumenical reconciler must first start with becoming reconciled with the chaplains he works with. Some of these other chaplains have been hurt deeply by the ignorant behavior and errant teachings of other faith groups. Those past experiences can leave deep scars. The chaplain as an ecumenical reconciler must be patient to ferret out what went wrong. He must read and study, from unbiased sources, the history of the offended chaplain's faith group. He must become familiar with their worship practices and sacred writings. His actions and words must always show respect. If the chaplain cannot show respect for another person's different teachings, how can the inmates be expected to be tolerant of other religions? Bias and prejudice were wrong in 1970. They are inexcusably wrong today.

We live in a pluralistic society. Each person has rights. Each person has responsibilities. The same is true for the religions of this country. There is a marketplace full of religious practices and teachings. While they may strongly differ among themselves about their various teachings and beliefs, they still have the right to exist without harassment.

In one prison where I worked, there was a faith group that came in every week and every week their leadership made it quite evident that I and my church were doomed to hell. One of the inmate workers in the Religious Services Center asked me why I put up with such abuse and treated these religious leaders so kindly. I told him it was a simple matter of showing them the respect that I would show the ministers of my own faith. It is my belief that the leaders of this faith group were acting out of spiritual ignorance and uninformed intellects. After two years of being subjected to their behavior, the chief representative of this faith group stopped me in the hallway one day and said, "We have noticed that you do not respond to us like other people do. We appreciate that. If there is anything we can do for you in the future, please feel free to ask."

An old saying states that ignorance is bliss. Ignorance is not bliss. Ignorance is hell. Anybody with a cursory knowledge of history can see that. This leads to another point that has been implied, but now needs to be said strongly.

The chaplain must first study the history of her own faith group. She must delve closely into the history of its leadership and the origins of its sacred writings and teachings. She must seek to read about her own faith group from sources other than her own teachers. The chaplain, as an educated person, must know that there is no such thing as a purely objective history of any subject. Nonetheless, the chaplain should seek out those historians who are widely respected in university circles, to read what they have to say about her faith group's teachings and foundation. She must seek to acknowledge the successes and failures of her faith group's leaders, members, teachings and practices.

If the chaplain comes from a faith group that is less than one hundred years old, he should proceed with great caution before he judges or presumes others to be wrong. If he is a student of history, which he should strive to become, he will note that all organizations, religious and secular, sooner or later will experience the pain of wounded human nature rising occasionally to the top.

Only after the chaplain has studied the history of his faith group, reading as many original documents and letters as possible, can he then read with perspective the history of those faith groups in which the inmates show an interest or to which they are affiliated. Study them all he must. Though he may not agree with their teachings, he should approach their practices and teachings with the same respect he would want for his own faith group. The more he keeps an attitude of respect as he studies the faith of other groups, he will discover the commonalities they all share.

For example, in 1974 I was fortunate to attend the first worldwide convocation of the bilateral theological dialogues that had been going on among five major denominations for ten years. One of the major themes of that week of sharing was the similarity of teachings we each could trace through the trajectories of history from the first century of Christianity to our modern era. When we put aside the narrow-minded approaches to history that were written along lines of a script that said, "My daddy is bigger than your daddy," we soon understood that we were more closely related as brothers and sisters than we first thought. That recognition may make some who are not very well educated feel a little uneasy. But the reality is that we have much more to rejoice in, when we objectively look at mankind's striving to serve God.

The chaplain as reconciler must do more than understand the commonalities of Christian history. She must strive to understand how some Christian teachings are culturally and sociologically conditioned. She must also devote energies to studying the other major faith groups of the world. As actively as she would attend convocations and seminars of other Christian denominations, she should do the same for Islam, Judaism, Hinduism, Buddhism, the mother earth religions, such as Wicca and Native Peoples, and the New Age religions. At the very, very minimum, if she considers some of these groups as lacking in truth, it is better the falsehood you know than the falsehood you don't know. However, it should be clearly stated that that attitude is not the ideal attitude. Again, it needs to be said: if these religions are approached with the same respect that is shown the Christian denominations, the chaplain will again come away with her own faith enriched. She will come away understanding that there is more that binds us as brother and sister creatures of God than divides us.

As the chaplain works actively to understand the religious practices and teachings of his fellow chaplains and volunteers, he must actively support and encourage the inmates in those practices. It is his ethical and moral obligation as a representative of the faith groups in civilian society. He represents more than his own denomination. Therefore, he should see to it that each faith group in the prison has equal opportunities to worship on their appointed days and to have time for religious education. As seriously as he would make efforts to have skilled volunteers work with the inmates of his own faith group, he has an ethical obligation to make those same efforts to contact and obtain support from mature and educated volunteers of the other faith groups.

Just as the chaplain would strive to have ideal worship and education equipment and supplies for her own faith group, such as robes, altar, candles, Bible study books, so she must strive to obtain the same or similar items for the other faith groups. To do less is unethical and unprofessional.

In a prison setting, the chaplain constantly must be aware of the limitations of time, space and practices imposed by virtue of that setting. All religions will find some limitations being imposed on them sooner or later by the nature of the place where they are. The chaplain must be knowledgeable of those limitations. She must never use her personal relationship with the governing authorities of the state to manipulate her way around those practices for the sake of her own faith group or any one faith group. If it is the policy of the government that food items not be brought in or delivered by outside faith groups, she must abide by that ruling equally for all. If it is the policy that the government permits only symbolic portions of alcoholic drink at worship services — e.g., communion wine for Catholics and glasses of wine for Jewish Passover, she must observe that policy equally for all. If it is the policy that inflammatory literature not be permitted into the institution, she must screen out those kinds of religious literature that attack other faith groups, whether the literature comes from her faith group or not.

When inmates come to the chaplain asking for a revival to be held outdoors, it is the obligation of the chaplain to inform those inmates that in a limited public area such a program could be violating the rights of other inmates to not be subjected to the teachings of the group conducting the revival. While it might be a common practice of a faith group to rent a vacant lot in a neighborhood to hold a revival, such circumstances do not automatically apply when there is a captive audience on government property. To take advantage of such circumstances to proselytize is unethical, immoral, unprofessional, and most likely would be viewed by the courts as an illegal conduct. None of these modes of conduct is ever proper for a chaplain to set as an example for those who are incarcerated for violating the rights of others.

The chaplain should be an active member of the team of employees who provide orientation programs for new inmates. As a member of that team it is her responsibility to encourage the inmates to become active in a faith group as a part of a well-balanced and developed life. It is an observable fact that those who maturely and with humility practice their faiths will seldom ever come back to prison. In this presentation and talk of encouragement, the chaplain must make it her obligation to see to it that all faith groups are spoken of with respect, and to teach the inmates that tolerance of differences is expected. She must strongly inform the inmates that being different is not the same as being wrong. She should point out that the same applies when speaking of racial groups or cultural practices.

When the chaplain is fortunate enough to have a budget, it is his obligation to see to it that each faith group has an equal opportunity to submit their ideal budget for the year. When the actual budget is determined, the paring down process should be done in consultation with each faith group's civilian representative in order to make sure that the cuts from the ideal to the real are in proper proportion for all. It is recommended that the inmates not be involved in this process. With their usually limited experience and educational backgrounds, they can too easily make groundless comparisons that can lead to animosity among the other groups of inmates. That animosity can lead to fighting on the yard or in the dormitories or cellblocks. It is the responsibility of the civilian leaders of those faith groups to tell their inmates that their needs were funded in the same proportion as the needs of the other faith groups. That is all that needs to be said.

When a chaplain leads or participates in a discussion group at the Religious Services Center, or anywhere else within the institution, she must make every effort to answer questions about practices and teachings of faith groups with accuracy, proper perspective and respect. If she does not know the answer to the question or problem proposed, it is her obligation to say so. Then she should consult with the proper authorities of that faith group for the correct answer and guidance. Only after that consultation should she then refer the correct information to the group in which or the person from which the question or problem arose.

If an inmate comes to the chaplain seeking information about a faith group other than the chaplain's, the chaplain has the obligation to provide objective and accurate information about the group and its teachings and practices. To provide biased information or incomplete information is unethical, immoral and unprofessional.

In the information racks in the hallway of the Religious Services Center, books and pamphlets and magazines from all of the faith groups should be given equal representation. The same is true for the bulletin board displays. To the degree that the chaplain can obtain such literature from the faith groups, for distribution or display, the items should be made equally available. Personal religious items such as rosaries, crosses, prayer beads, medals and chains, Bibles and Korans, if they are permitted by the government, should be given with ease of access to members of all faith groups.

If an inmate dies, and none of his relatives can be found or the relatives do not wish to take the responsibility for burying the body, it is the moral obligation of the chaplain to ascertain the faith background of the inmate. Then the chaplain should make arrangements for a burial service in accordance with the teachings of the inmate's faith group. The chaplain should make every effort to find a representative of that faith group to preside at the grave side service.

It is the duty of the chaplain to inform his institution's administrators of the various burial customs of each faith group, and to see that those customs are respected. In those institutions where the inmate choir cannot go outside the fence to provide music for the service, when music should be a customary part of the funeral and burial rite, the chaplain should make every effort to obtain volunteers from community congregations to provide that service. Where it is the custom to provide flowers at a grave side, the chaplain should obtain funds from his budget or from volunteers to provide at least a modest symbol of the custom.

When there are seasons of fasting and public penance for various faith groups, it is the responsibility of the chaplain to consult authorities in those faith groups to see what accommodations they will make for their adherents who are in prison. Having negotiated those guidelines with the religious leaders, it is then the responsibility of the chaplain to communicate those needs to the prison administrators to see that those practices are permitted in the widest sense possible. If it is necessary for the chaplain to change his work schedule to accommodate those practices, it is his duty to do so.

In those cases where prison administrators make decisions that impinge upon the religious practices of any of the faith groups, it is the obligation of the chaplain to accurately, fairly and firmly defend the faith group's right to practice their religion without undue interference. For example, at one prison where I worked, it was the custom of the maintenance department to complete all work orders from the chapel on Friday afternoons. Since the noise and confusion was in direct conflict with Islamic Juma, the main worship service of the week for the Islamic Community, I had to negotiate with the warden and the deputy warden for a different day for the completion of work orders at the chapel.

On another occasion, the recreation department scheduled championship play for baseball and football on Sunday mornings. Saturday afternoons were equally available. I negotiated with the recreation supervisor for a change of schedule. After that negotiation experience, the recreation supervisor started attending Sunday Protestant services in the chapel.

On those occasions when the notorious leaders of faith groups are publicly charged and convicted of illegal or immoral conduct, it is the role of the chaplain to honestly acknowledge the offenses of the individuals and to counsel the inmates that the notorious leaders do not represent all the members of that faith group. In no manner, shape or form may the chaplain ever glory in the downfall of other religious leaders. Since he should know history, he should know better. His is the primary role to put all things into proper perspective.

When audio/visual equipment is purchased, it is the chaplain's duty to see that it is available and equally accessible to all faith groups. The principle of screening out inflammatory tapes and movies applies here the same as it does for printed material. However, the fact that the chaplain may disagree with the content of the teaching contained in the tapes or movies is not grounds to refuse their hearing or showing.

At those times when the chaplain presides over the worship services and religious education classes of his own faith group, he will naturally provide those services as the pastor of that group. At all times when he is ministering to individuals or groups, he should treat them with utmost civility, dignity, respect and honor.

When an inmate comes to the chaplain to request admission into a faith group through initiation rites, it is never ethical for a chaplain to question that decision or request. It is the responsibility of the chaplain to arrange for authorized civilian leaders of that group to come to the prison to perform the ceremony in the manner that is appropriate to the security of the institution.

If the chaplain cannot be comfortable living her faith in the presence of other faith groups, she may seriously need to examine the commitment she has to her own faith group. If her faith is easily threatened by the presence of the religious teachings and practices of others, her own commitment may not be very firm. Before she accuses others, let her examine herself. If she finds that she cannot show respect and fairness to other religions in a prison setting, she needs to leave the prison ministry and seek a ministerial setting elsewhere in her denomination.

CHAPTER SIX

THE CHAPLAIN AS COUNSELOR

"Chaplain, come here a minute. I need to talk to you." The sixty-five-year-old, gray-haired surgeon grabbed me by the arm and ushered me into the hospital supply room. It was the nearest door. I had been ordained a little over two years. I had been in that city for only two months and was making rounds in the small community hospital as chaplain of the week. The surgeon had been in the community as a highly-respected professional for over thirty years. But length of years and length of service were not on his mind that afternoon. He wanted to talk about the grief process for the surviving family members and himself. He wanted to talk.

He could have called one of the psychiatrists in the medical building next door to make an appointment. But the issue at hand was not about idiopathic behavior. It was not about psychotic behavior. He could not wait for a one hour appointment one week from now. His issue was about life and death, an issue we all face and deal with in our lives. He needed to talk about his own perspective; his own role in a plan that was bigger than man. He needed to talk about a plan that, at the gut level, most of mankind calls divine.

As an active member of his own faith group, the surgeon

understood that we are confronted with a large degree of mystery when we attempt to peer into the reasons for life and death. He also knew that at their roots life and death issues were connected with the experience of love. At that moment that afternoon he knew he needed to be connected once again to the source of mystery. He knew he needed to be reconnected in more than just his mind. He needed the re-connection through the sharing of another human being. He needed to share with another human being who was striving to live life through the perspective of faith.

The surgeon knew and saw all of that in the instant when he saw the clerical collar. He knew and saw that within twenty minutes an empathetic ear and shared prayer would get him started back on the road to living out his vocation as a Christian surgeon.

The chaplain as counselor in a prison setting carries out much the same role with the inmates that the surgeon was looking for. She serves in moments of crisis as a listener, a gentle guide, a path finder, and a connector and reassurer of things divine.

Through the years of her training, the chaplain should have taken many courses in psychology at the undergraduate and graduate level. She should have taken and become experienced in a number of psychological testing programs. It should have been her experience to be involved in group therapy work as well, both as a participant and as a leader. She should have been experienced in compiling verbatims and keeping records.

Her training and experience should have included all of this before ordination, so that she can clearly know more about who she is and who she is not. She needs to know when to make referrals for deeply-rooted psychotic behavior, and she needs to know when it is appropriate to work as a member of the mental health team. She needs to know when the pastoral insight is called for and appropriate. She needs to know that she is not a psychologist, nor a psychiatrist. She needs to know that she is a pastor. She needs to know that a major part on her role is to help the inmates discover whose they are, as well as who they are.

The fifty minute model for most counseling sessions is a rarity for the chaplain. The five to ten minutes of crisis counseling is more common. While a private practitioner may have a case load of twenty to forty clients a week, an active chaplain may have ten to twenty "clients" a day, in between scheduled worship services and religious education classes.

It is not uncommon to have a sequence of inmates come to the chaplain with the following sorts of problems.

1. "I tried to cut my wrists last night in the shower room at 4:00 A.M., but my bunkie caught me and helped me clean up the mess. The guards don't know about it."
2. "I just called home and found out my three-year-old daughter was burned over sixty percent of her body in a house fire."
3. "I go up for parole next month, and my mother tells me I can't come home."
4. "I just went to the parole board, and they told me I have to step off another five years."
5. "My wife hasn't been down to visit me for three months because she doesn't have a car. Her sister usually drives her, but she had a nervous breakdown."
6. "My son just got arrested for breaking and entering."
7. "What does Joshua, Chapter 11, really mean? We had a fight over it in the dorm last night."
8. "I go to the parole board in three months, and my wife just wrote me that she is filing for divorce."

9. "How can you tell if you are doing God's will?"

10. "When I came in here last month to talk to you about why I was in prison, it was all a lie."

11. "Chaplain, this is the warden's office. We need you to tell inmate Jones that his sister was shot three times in the back of the head and killed."

12. "Teach me how to pray."

13. "I have been raped three times in the past month, and I am tired of being someone's 'boy toy.'"

14. "Some punk disrespected me last night, and I didn't go off on him, because I was trying to practice my faith. Now I feel terrible, like I've lost my manhood."

15. "I keep having these visions that God is calling me to start a neighborhood community center after I get released."

16. "I used to be into Satanism, and I can't get the pictures of all the blood out of my mind."

17. "I can't got to church anymore, because when I was in Vietnam I saw a chaplain get the top of his head blown off by a sniper during Mass. I was next to him, when it happened."

18. "What is the correct Bible to read?"

19. " I keep hearing these voices, and they won't stop."

20. "There's forty gallons of hooch in my dorm, and they're going to bring it out tonight for a party."

21. "I've just found Jesus and want to be a minister."

22. "Chaplain, this is the warden's office calling. We have another death message for you."

The above combination of problems does not begin to cover all the types of problems, questions, and crises that come to the chaplain in the course of one day. But the variety is certainly not unusual. However, the chaplain is expected to handle it all and have an answer for each one. He is expected to have an answer that is honest, compassionate, knowledgeable, inspiring and prayerful.

When an inmate comes in with visions of grandeur for his parole plan, the chaplain has to confront him with the limitations of reality. When the inmate comes to tell the chaplain that all his (the inmate's) problems are the fault of everybody else, the chaplain has to question the inmate about his vision of responsibility. He has to challenge him at that moment, face to face. When the inmate comes to say that his "woman" won't follow his orders, the chaplain must speak the truth about human relationships and correct interpretations of the Bible.

When an inmate comes to the chaplain to say that his dog of fourteen years has died, the chaplain must offer a compassionate ear to the reality that an important part of that man's life has died, and the inmate has no one to understand his pain.

When an inmate comes in to be told that two of his children and a niece and nephew were killed in a house fire, the chaplain has to allow the man to cry and scream and curse and pound on the furniture. The chaplain has to stay with him through the shock and offer appropriate physical touch, an action that is normally forbidden in prison.

When an inmate comes in with a question, problem, or a challenge about religion, the chaplain must know what he is talking about and where to find the proper references. The chaplain must have his facts straight. To most inmates, the chaplain is the absolute certain voice of God in matters religious and spiritual. On the other hand, the chaplain knows most certainly he is not the absolute voice of God. He is in sales. God is in management. But the reality is that the inmates' expectations and perspectives are not matched with ordinary reality. An incorrect or biased answer from the chaplain can lead the inmate to a behavior that can cause a fight or near riot in the dorm.

The chaplain must not only be knowledgeable about a host of religious practices and teachings, he must have the art of communicating and counseling with that knowledge in a manner that is appropriate to the best norms and traditions of the religion in question. He must be able to counsel and advise the inmate about which religious practices are permitted in a prison setting, which are not, and why.

When an inmate comes in to struggle with the spiritual dimensions of depression, the chaplain has to recognize the depth of the struggle. She should consult with the psychologist and psychiatrist to determine what counseling programs and medications are available for the inmate. At the same time, the chaplain needs to find those portions of the sacred writings of the inmate's faith group that refer to hope and forgiveness and acceptance. If he is Christian, it may help the inmate if the chaplain can relate the message of the Book of Job, or the Book of Hosea, along with other passages and books, whose themes are built around hope, forgiveness, and acceptance. Further, the chaplain needs to expose the inmate to the spiritually healthy benefits of meditation, as well as vigorous physical exercise.

For example, for many months I worked with an inmate who could find no purpose in his life, who could not believe that God could forgive his sins, and who felt that he could never be loved. We met every other week for a half hour. Finally one day he rose from his chair, came straight for me without saying a word, dropped to his knees and grabbed me by the shoulders. Then he rested his head on my shoulder and sobbed for fifteen minutes. When he stood, my shirt was soaked. Some months later, as he was leaving for parole, he came to my office to say goodbye. His last words were, "Whose shoulder can I find to cry on now?" In the intervening months, he had grown to understand his faults, his limits, God's forgiveness and the saving grace of self love. The inmate left seven years ago. He has not come back to prison, yet. Hopefully, our teamwork — the psychologist, the psychiatrist, and the chaplain — did the man some good, enough good to enable him to function outside the cocoon of a prison.

When an inmate comes into the office to confess that he has raped somebody, or stolen another's property, or cheated on his wife, the chaplain must understand the sacramentality of the moment. She must understand the need for healing grace to be offered, when she perceives that the inmate is truly repentant for the hurt he has caused others. She needs to know when to offer prayer, especially the prayer of absolution in the name of the faith community and in the name of God.

When a man comes in to say that everybody has told him he is no good and will never amount to anything, the chaplain needs to offer inspiring words of encouragement, encouragement that is realistic. In the course of a conversation in my office one day, an inmate said, "I have always been told that I am a slow learner." From the context and content of his conversation up to that point, I was able to respond, "No, Jim. You are not a slow learner. You are a late learner." With that Jim left my office and went straight to the school office to register. In six months, he had his G.E.D. and had applied for a loan to go to college. Within four months after he was paroled, he was a full-time student at a prestigious university.

On another occasion, an inmate had attempted suicide. After the correctional officer cut him down, the inmate crawled under the steel shelf that served as his bed. It was bolted to the wall. He grabbed hold of the support posts. When all humane attempts had failed to dislodge him, the shift captain's office called for me to see if I could do anything to help. (Notice that the chaplain was called last. That is not an unusual circumstance.

In a prison setting, a chaplain has to be used to being thought of as a last resort, if at all, in moments of crisis.) After talking to the inmate for a few minutes and getting no response, I got down on the floor and placed my body parallel to his. I was about two inches away from him. He turned his head and looked at me, eyeball to eyeball. I said to him, "Isn't this the craziest damn thing you've ever seen?" He laughed. I invited him to my office for a cup of coffee. He came. On the way out of the cell, I told the shift captain we'd be ready to meet with him at the chapel in about an hour.

There is an old saying that if you expect the miraculous, you must be willing to do the ridiculous. To the people in civilian society, it is ridiculous to think that five or ten minute counseling sessions can accomplish anything or do any good. The reality is that God can use the human instrument to do the miraculous. The chaplain as counselor must never lose sight of his instrumentality.

There will also be times when staff members will come to the chaplain for counseling. They may have marital problems. They may have problems with alcohol, problems with a common law wife, or problems with drugs. They may have been sexually abused as children and are now involved in abusing someone else. They may have problems with financial management, or their immediate supervisor at the institution. They may be involve in criminal behavior with an inmate, or they may be wrestling with the problem of which faith to follow in an active way. All of these problems are real and serious. They have a direct impact on the employee "family." These employees are members of the team with the chaplain. They play a supportive role in the rehabilitation of the inmate. However, as much as the chaplain may want to counsel with these employees, she must recognize her limitations. She was hired to work with and for the inmates. The employees may have pastors of choice in their communities. The inmates have only one or two choices.

In cases of employee problems, it is the primary goal of the chaplain to maintain confidentiality and to direct the employee to solidly professional and responsible sources of counseling in the employee's home community. The chaplain should keep in mind the resources of the church to which the employee may belong. Above all, the chaplain should be in contact with the representative of the employee assistance program and stay currently knowledgeable of the resources available through that avenue.

The chaplain should also be aware of what her legal limits and responsibilities are. Just as she should be professional enough to know when to make a referral for an inmate to other professional resources, she cannot afford to think that she can handle the emotional and legal problems of the staff as well. Again, it is not that she doesn't care. However, with a compassionate heart, she must recognize that the inmates are her primary parishioners and direct the staff to other pastors in the community.

In order that the chaplain keep a proper perspective about her role and function, it is essential that she join with other clergy persons, whether in the chaplaincy or not, for regular sessions of sharing frustrations, insights, successes and prayer. Without such a professional support group, a chaplain can become a dry and ineffective instrument of God or easily burn out.

I am reminded of a time when a handful of inmates were asking for sponsorship of a prayer group. I was not personally in favor of the type of prayer group they were asking for. However, in other prisons it had done no harm. After three months of discussion and planning, I scheduled the meeting time for the group at 8:15 A.M. on Saturday morning. This was the only time slot open in my schedule. Thinking that only three or four of the eight inmates, who had requested the group prayer, would show up for the first session, I was quite surprised when nearly twenty men came to pray that first morning. When I mentioned this to the group, one man immediately said, "See what happens when you do the right thing."

Whether or not the warden permits the chaplain to arrange his schedule to attend a support group, the chaplain must make time for such activity in his life. He must make attendance at such a group a top priority of his spiritual and professional life. It is the right thing to do. Or, as an old Latin proverb is translated, "You cannot give what you don't have."

CHAPTER SEVEN

THE CHAPLAIN AS PASTORAL ADMINISTRATOR

Working in a non-supportive secular environment, with lack of adequate staff, the chaplain performs administrative duties to a degree that community clergy would find intolerable.

There has always been tension between the goals and purposes of a prison. The first goal is the obvious intent of society, when it passes laws to restrict aberrant behavior that society believes threatens its security. Therefore, by law the offending person is isolated from the normal intercourse of society. Or to put it another way, society sends a person to prison as punishment. The prisoner is not sent to prison *for* punishment. From this statement comes the other point that makes the tension. What do you do with a person while she is in prison? Is it enough to lock her up and feed her? Will that in itself bring about a correction of behavior that will restore her to a productive and responsible role in society? This other prong of the tension states that we must do something with the inmate while she is incarcerated, that will bring about a positive change in her life. Most people call this rehabilitation.

The nub of the problem is that most state agencies are painfully aware of society's expectations for the agency to operate within its budget. Never mind that the number of people being served has increased. Never mind that wages have to keep pace with inflation so that the agency will be able to draw trained persons from the existing labor pool. Hence, most administrators of prisons will, of necessity, direct the largest portion of their budget to the cost of confining the inmates. When they send their budget requests to the governor and the legislature, it is almost an embarrassment for them to tag on to the requests some money for treatment services, for rehabilitation. There is usually a reluctant acknowledgment that the "do-gooders" of society do raise a fuss unless some bones are thrown in the direction of programs that try to change the lives of the inmates. Most governors and legislators reflect the mistaken belief that punishment and harsh living will motivate an inmate enough so that he will not come back to prison. They do not take into account that pent-up rage may also be a motivator.

With the attitude of the governors, legislators, and the directors of departments of corrections being one of reluctance to spend money on treatment services, it becomes obvious to the rising bureaucrat at the bottom of the heap, that the way to his rising up the career ladder lies through a mentality of lock-and-feed. A "good bureaucrat" will not see his career advancing through programs that change peoples' behaviors. We just might have to close some prisons and the "good bureaucrat" might find himself without a job.

So then, in a prioritizing mode at which all "good bureaucrats" become skilled, it becomes obvious that the few bones that are being thrown into the treatment area should be spent in such a way as to cause the least amount of conflict among the staff and among the inmates, and in such a way that the expenditure will achieve the greatest amount of public relations. The fact that something may be good for an inmate in his total development does not matter.

Hence, in our scientific, technical culture, psychological testing, which purports to be a measurable science until you talk to more than one psychologist, is seen as a program to which you can throw a bone and get some positive public relations at the same time. Once more, it does not matter that most prison psychologists are really psychology assistants and not board-certified licensed psychologists.

The next program area that is being pushed as having a positive influence on the rehabilitation of the whole person is recreation. That is the intended public relations purpose for recreation programs. A former director of corrections once put it far more truthfully and bluntly. He said that if he had an extra one hundred thousand dollars in his budget, he would put every dime of it into recreation programs, because he could "get more bang for the buck." He said he could get more men involved per dollar spent. He could keep more people occupied.

The problem is that most recreational activities in a prison are not in areas that most convicts will be involved in, when they get released from prison. How often will their work hours make it possible for them to gather nine other friends and acquaintances to play basketball, or seventeen other persons to play baseball? Most of the activities that the inmates are involved in are never supervised. The interpersonal interactions are never discussed or thought through. Most of what takes place are the same sort of unsupervised and unorganized activities you find ten-year-old boys engaged in at the corner sand lot.

There can be six employees in the recreation department. Four will be involved with paperwork. Two will be involved with the inmates. But because society believes that recreation is a good thing, and because the newspapers and television stations can be called upon to cover an occasional specific event, the smart administrator knows that it will further his career to prioritize the recreation programs and get positive publicity for his institution.

In recent decades it has become common knowledge that the vast majority of inmates are under-educated. Thus, some tax money has been allocated in an attempt to build accredited school systems in prison. While the majority in the system are good teachers, it happens too often that there is no teacher present in the classroom. At other times, teachers read personal books at the desk. Because of the lack of funds for first-rate teaching materials, the textbooks and what is taught from them are usually out of date. It is common knowledge among the inmates that if they get an "A" in the prison school, it is equivalent to a "C" in secular society. The standards have been dropped to make the bureaucrat look successful.

Finally, as important as the last flea on the last hair on the tail of the dog, religion comes into the mix of treatment programs. Because of a past history of political friends being hired as chaplains in the prison system, the chaplaincy itself has an image as a refuge for the woefully-undereducated and somewhat pious nice guys, who "know the Word." In addition, it is accepted knowledge that a number of denominations permit some of their clergy to work in prisons, because some of them are misfits in the civilian community. Thus, it doesn't take a smart administrator long to determine who will get the crumbs when it comes to budgetary support. If he needs a further excuse, he can always use the cloud that hangs over the interpretation of church/state involvement.

Hence, it takes little imagination to understand why the professional religious staff in a state prison setting is normally only forty percent of what would be considered basic by federal prison standards. That does not count support staff, of which there is none. For a profession, whose main tool of trade is words and the communication of them, it is almost unheard of for a chaplain to have even a token of secretarial support. It is never heard of that a chaplain would have a civilian Director of Religious Education, or a full-time musician, or a paid civilian choir director.

The chaplain as a pastoral administrator must rely on inmates for staff support. Though many inmates often lack even the basic skills for spelling and grammar, they do the best they can to be of service to the chaplains and the inmates, who worship at the Religious Services Center. Seldom have the inmate helpers had any experience at using a word processor or a computer. If they have had any skills at answering a telephone in a business setting, they are not allowed to answer the phone, anyway. But, again, in their hearts they understand the chaplain's need for support staff and offer what skills they have for the good of the believing community. So, the chaplain must be patient to spend months training the inmate support staff to do the simplest secretarial functions.

Unfortunately, after spending months training the inmate, he is usually transferred off the job by the Office of Inmate Personnel, or sent to another institution, or paroled a few months later. It is a constant revolving door that eats up the time the chaplain should be spending being a pastor. Yet, the chaplain's ability to function as a pastor would be hampered to an even greater degree without inmate help. The average inmate staff person works at the Religious Services Center about six to nine months. The fact that this working arrangement takes away from the chaplain's time to perform the religious and counseling functions of a trained professional is of little or no concern to the prison administration. Because the prison administrator inherited the situation, it has never occurred to him that it can be or should be any different. This same lack of creative thinking exists in other areas of the responsibilities of the chaplain as administrator.

Other than inmate janitorial help, there is no maintenance staff for the Religious Services Center. What maintenance work needs to be done has to be the job of the chaplain as administrator to coordinate on his own. There is no building or maintenance committee that he can refer to or use to supervise his inmate janitorial staff. Again, recognizing the position of religion on the totem pole of priorities, it takes little imagination to understand how quickly the maintenance department of the prison is going to respond to the needs of the Religious Services Center.

For example, the cleaning of the fans is a normal maintenance function. To clean a fan, a screwdriver is often needed to remove the protective shield. A screwdriver in a prison is a contraband item, because it can be used as a weapon. Thus, a request has to be made to the maintenance department to send up a civilian staff person with a screwdriver to remove the shield. As the chaplain administrator, I filled out a work order and sent it to the deputy warden, who oversees the maintenance department. Two weeks later I received my work order request form back with a note attached, saying, "You used the wrong form." The only form I was ever told to use for maintenance work was a work order form. So I called the deputy. He was not available. After calling three times over a five day period and leaving messages for him to return my call, the deputy's secretary told me I needed a tool request form. Since I did not have such a form, she offered to send me some.

A week later I received the forms and filled one out immediately, again sending it to the deputy. Two weeks later I received the form with a note attached, saying, "You filled this out wrong." After calling the secretary, I found out that I had neglected to fill in one line of the form. Having completed the form "properly," I returned it to the deputy. One week later a civilian maintenance person, escorting an inmate worker, came to the Religious Services Center with a screwdriver. The inmate removed the protective shield. My inmate janitor cleaned the blades. The inmate maintenance staff person replaced the shield. It took twenty minutes to do a job that it took six weeks to arrange.

Or again, when we moved the Religious Services Department into a former weight lifting room, we wanted to paint it so it would be presentable as a worship hall. We were told there was no money for paint. So we spoke to some Pentecostal pastors, who donated eight hundred dollars' worth of paint and supplies. They even offered to supply the labor to complete the task. The warden said he would accept the supplies and paint, but not the offer of free labor. Eighteen months later the maintenance department sent a crew to paint the worship hall and other areas in the Religious Services Center. Over that eighteen month period, the warden had given his solemn word five times that the center would be painted in the next thirty days. Because the lower staff within the institution knew that religion did not register on the list of priorities throughout the entire prison system, they blithely ignored the warden. They knew he really didn't mean what he said to us. By the time the maintenance crew got around to painting the chapel, one-third of all our custom-blended paints and one half of our supplies had been stolen from the maintenance storage areas, where everything is supposed to be kept under lock and key. The unique colors we had chosen for the Religious Services Center were seen in dorm areas, recreation areas, work areas, and offices throughout the institution.

Five years later, when the institution offered to repaint our center, the maintenance staff told us they would have the job finished in two weeks. We rescheduled worship groups to accommodate the paint crew. Five months later the paint crew picked up their tarps and equipment and left. They left behind some paint for the chapel inmate staff to finish the job. The quality of the work done by the maintenance crew was such that most civilians would refuse to pay a painter for such a mess.

Or again, at any prison there will be some deaths occurring due to natural causes in the course of a year. At the prison, where I have most recently worked, because of the make-up of our populations, deaths occur more frequently. Because the governors and directors and the legislators have not made it known that they consider religious services as an integral part of prison life, the notion of neglect filters down to the local level. Because of this, an inmate can be dead a week before the chaplain is ever notified about it by the warden's office.

Usually, the chaplains hear about the death of an inmate through the inmate grapevine. When the chaplain brings this lack of professional courtesy to the warden's and deputy warden's attention and asks to be put on the notification list, the request is conveniently ignored. After working with five wardens over a period of ten years and bringing the problem to the attention of each of them, we were still not notified in a timely fashion when an inmate died. It is most awkward for the chaplain to receive a call from the family of the recently-deceased inmate and not know that the man died.

These are just a few of the examples of what a chaplain as an administrator has to work with in a non-supportive secular environment. Time and time again the chaplain is left off the list of inter-office routing of communiques. Time and time again the chaplain has to remind the warden and the deputies that he should be included on those routing lists. About a year ago, a regional director issued a letter referring to departmental policy about religious diets. The policy had been written two years ago. The chaplains did not receive a copy of it. The inmates had read about it in the law library. After notifying the warden's office that the original policy had never been sent to the chaplains, the policy arrived at the chaplains' office nine days later. The clergy person in a community setting is working with a group of people that have one common goal, the communication of a life of faith. The chaplain as administrator has to understand that his goal does not register on the scale of concerns or interests for the majority of bureaucrats.

In a setting where a community congregation would have five full-time clergy persons, three secretaries, two directors of religious education and a full-time musician, the prison staff may include two full-time clergy persons and an occasional part-time contract person. If the chaplain has any civilian support committee and staff, it is on his time away from the ministry at the prison.

Attending staff meetings, supervising inmate staff, hiring inmate staff, answering telephones, sorting, opening and reading mail, and providing security coverage for religious programs can consume fifty percent of a chaplain's time. Somewhere in the midst of all these activities, a chaplain is supposed to keep the individual files on each of the inmates in the institution, noting the inmate's religious preference, and keeping a log of any and all transactions that take place between the chaplain and the inmate. In a prison of 2,500 inmates, about thirteen hundred a year will leave and thirteen hundred new men will arrive. Old files have to be emptied and new files made. There is no secretarial help to assist with this task. Then, somewhere in the midst of all of her pastoral responsibilities the chaplain has to be the purchasing agent for all the items approved for the budget. The layers of paperwork to purchase even the simplest item can consume hours of precious time.

As though all the above were not enough, the paperwork to arrange for a volunteer to come to the prison to provide a free service for one of the faith groups can take a week or more to clear all the hurdles. Again, the chaplain has no one to help with the paperwork. Then, to cap it all off monthly reports must be filled out; telephone logs of all long distance calls must be filled out and submitted each month — in minute detail; an updated inventory of all equipment and furniture must be submitted each year; and an annual report is required. If central office decides to do a survey of volunteer services, or of minority services, or whatever is the topic of the hour, the chaplain as the administrator has to find time somewhere to process this paperwork on her own. In the meantime, the people-work, for which she was hired, has to wait.

The chaplain as administrator not only has to have the patience of Job, he has to be willing to be a jack-of-all-trades and skills, knowing that some administrative functions are necessary if the religious services program are going to exist at all. But the overload of all the incidental administrative functions that could be done by someone with a basic high school education adds tension to his primary calling to be a pastor to the inmates.

When we started a religious services program at one prison, I discovered that we had no budget. I called another chaplain at another prison and found out that he had been granted a total of thirty dollars the previous year for his budget. Astoundingly, he was happy with that. He, too, had been granted no budget for the current year.

As a result of having no budget, the two of us chaplains went to churches in the area to give thirty talks that year. All on our own time we gave talks about our prison ministry and begged for physical and financial support. We collected desks, file cabinets, typewriters and chairs, clocks and hymnals, and a pulpit and an altar. The state did provide us with a telephone and installed it on a wall where a desk would not fit.

Over the next six years, we were able to get the state to give us money to provide for some of our programs. That money came from a fund that one of the chaplains had started at another prison. It was not tax money; not state budget money. But money, nonetheless. Then during the next three years those funds were reduced to the point that it was not possible to expand our programs without the help of our civilian supporters. The bottom line is that the chaplain as administrator is in a non-supportive environment where he must be willing to work overtime, or accept the reality of having little or no programs to serve the extensive spiritual needs of the inmates.

In a private survey, it was found that about one in five wardens is active in some faith group and that about eighty percent of prison employees are divorced persons. This does not mean that they do not have a sense of faith in God. However, it usually means that they do not have a clue about which administrative responsibilities of a clergy person are supported by a community congregation. Thus, the prison administrators do not act out of anger, when they deprive the chaplain of ordinary administrative support. Rather, they act out of benign, ignorant indifference. The chaplain as administrator has to know this and understand that the indifference and non-support is not directed at her personally. The bureaucrats around her do not know any better. They certainly have not been instructed by their central office authority figures that they should know better. Again, the chaplain as administrator must remember that she is tolerated on the institution's table of organization, because a few people fear that working without a chaplain on the organizational chart might cause a few people in civilian circles to be upset.

The chaplain as administrator needs to be patient with the style of prison administration. While there are management training programs in some prison systems, they are usually in-house generated. Frequently, they have no infusion of outside information about what styles of management are being taught in accredited business colleges. While physical inbreeding produces imbeciles, inbred prison training leads to some interesting management aberrations.

For example, one warden I worked with was proud of the fact that his management style could be summed up in the following way. "I don't get ulcers; I give ulcers." The fact that there might be a constructive alternative had never occurred to him. It was never evident that he understood that he saw his employees as human beings, either. That same warden said loudly and clearly that he never wanted to hear any of his employees say that they had to see the doctor about, or take pills for, or be hospitalized for stress. In a firm and most authoritative edict he declared, "There is no such thing as stress." He was not joking. He was on his way up the career ladder to a position in central office. The fact that his management style was pitiful seemed never to have dawned on to him or his superiors.

Another warden in recent years arranged the furniture in his office so that all the other chairs in the room were lower than his. His high-backed chair simulated a throne. He presided from behind the desk, a desk that was the largest piece of furniture in the room. The fact that the arrangement of his furniture was communicating a style of management-by-intimidation did not seem to occur to him. I have visited ten wardens in the last five years, who use this style of management-by-intimidation. I have met only one warden in that same period, who is sensitive to the latest teaching on management styles.

The chaplain as administrator has to be aware of the ignorance of more humane styles of management by prison administrators. The chaplain has to be patient that the management styles she has learned at accredited schools have not yet penetrated the protective cocoon of prison management. The chaplain has to be willing to work in a primitive and certainly non-religious administrative environment, If she doesn't have the tolerance for petty games and planned ignorance, she should not consider this her calling. One chaplain, who could not tolerate such non-supportive ignorance, chose not to leave. Instead, she chose to do nothing but sit in her office and read books. She provided three very minimal worship services a week. She has been among the living dead ever since.

Another example of a non-supportive secular environment is the scheduling of group recreation activities on Sunday mornings. The warden and his recreation staff could not see how such scheduling was communicating to the inmates that religion was not an important part of life. The chaplain as administrator has to schedule his programs knowing that he is up against competition that his partners in the civilian community have not yet had to bear in an ever deadening secular environment.

Or again, at one prison where I worked there was no Religious Services Center. Worship was scheduled in the library. But the regular library operations were not shut down. We had to endure staff and inmates talking in regular volumes while we tried to pray. At the same institution, we had to schedule our large, group worship services in the gymnasium. If our service ran one minute over the one hour allotted time, the staff recreation leaders would give basketballs to waiting inmates and encourage them to dribble the balls, so that we would get the message to get out. For small worship groups and religious education classes we had to use school classrooms. The problem was that from the neighboring classrooms up and down the hall emanated a volume of noise so loud that the religious leaders of the groups could hardly hear themselves think.

The chaplain as administrator has to be creative, patient, tolerant, and imaginative. She has to be certain in the core of her being that she is not called to ministerial fulfillment with the civilian staff, but with the inmates whom she was first called to serve. The inmates need the example of faith lived through trying circumstances. The chaplain as administrator must also see that there is a pastoral role of witness she is giving as she lives through a lot of secular nonsense.

The chaplain as administrator will find that there are a few faith-filled people in administrative positions. These people will be a quiet support for the chaplain. At the same time, the chaplain as administrator needs to know that these staff persons pay the price of ridicule every time they are caught helping him. Such circumstances follow the old law of economics — there is no such thing as a free lunch. Those people, who work in the business office, maintenance, custody or administrative positions, have to call in favors every time they help the chaplain. This costs them on their jobs. These people are reenacting the role of Joseph of Arimathea by their quiet, behind the scenes support. The chaplain as administrator needs to be aware of the price these people pay for befriending him. In turn, he needs to be supportive of them and their pastoral needs. Besides praying for them daily, he needs to let them know verbally that he deeply appreciates their sacrifices.

In the Gospel according to Matthew (10:16), Jesus tells his followers to be as clever as snakes and gentle as doves when dealing with the people of the world. The chaplain as administrator must know the basic principles and practices of good business management. But she must also be strong enough in her faith commitment not to be sucked into the game playing of our modern secular managers, who will walk over and do in anyone who gets in their way, as they climb the career ladder to the elusive thrill of power. The chaplain generates her gentleness and ability not to be fazed by manipulators from her prayer life, from her relationship to God, the only true source of fulfilling power.

CHAPTER EIGHT

THE CHAPLAIN AS PROPHET

The chaplain is *called to live out the ancient religious role of the one who speaks for the inmates on behalf of the church to the government in those areas that affect justice, ethics, morals, and the religious and civil rights of women and men.* This is a role for which there is no comparison in the other professions. This is because the chaplain is the only one who can give these areas of concern a religious dimension. All the others, such as institutional inspector, carry out their role in the secular sense of the ombudsman.

Called:

The discernment of whether or not the chaplain is speaking for himself or God through the church is never an easy thing to do. Nor was it an easy thing to do when the prophets in ancient history spoke out. The one who was called was not called to be a fortune teller or future teller or some sort of soothsayer. From the earliest religious history the essence of a prophet was to be the one who was called to be a spokesman for God in those matters that concerned God's will. Most usually, this entailed the prophet's fulfilling the role of calling mankind back to a right relationship with God.

That was never a popular job. Hence, the one called often

tried to refuse the call. A prophet nearly always pays a price for speaking out for God. Most ancient prophets were killed or, at the very least, exiled from the community to whom they had been sent to serve.

In more modern times, prophets are either fired, censored or transferred. Sometimes they are sent to psychiatric centers so that their message may be discredited. At other times, depending on the form of government tyranny, they are assassinated. An ancient Turkish proverb says it well: "He who would tell the truth should keep one foot in the stirrup."

Because human nature is wounded by sin, there will always be the need for someone to be called to be a spokesman to call us back to do God's will. It is historically evident that governments and churches need to be called back to the Truth regularly. As we all know, power corrupts, and absolute power corrupts absolutely. Both state and church are two organizations that naturally tend to wield absolute power.

For discernment of the truth, it is incumbent upon the chaplain to have a spiritual mentor or mentors. She should have a spiritual guide or belong to a prayer group of other clergy persons who meet on a weekly or nearly weekly basis. The chaplain needs a spiritually mature person or persons to whom she can speak in full confidence to discern what it is she is experiencing and how best to respond as God would will.

Once more we are dealing in an area for which the state makes no reimbursement for time spent in direct relationship to maintaining an essential skill as a chaplain. It is not unusual for this sort of spiritual guidance and shared prayer to take an average of three hours a week. This is time spent outside the forty hours on the job and time away from family and friends. This is not personal time. This is professional time. This is time that is essential to keeping unredeemed personality traits out of the reach of interfering in the search for truth. A true prophet is one who does not necessarily want to give the message, to be the spokesperson, but feels impelled by a call from God to fulfill this role. While there is always a price to pay, the chaplain as prophet invests her time in spiritual development to be able to pay the price.

To live out the ancient religious role:
The role has been discussed above. What needs to be added is that the prophet always lived out the role in a spirit of humble service. He was never one who first rose to a position of power and then sought to smite those who were abusing him or his people.

The truthfulness and simplicity of his style of life were seen as marks that he was really called. It would be hard to picture John the Baptist driving a "pimpmobile" or wearing silk suits or being the presiding judge for any particular religious party. The chaplain must not give in to a desire for a lifestyle that others with his comparable training attempt to live. Materialistic showmanship and political coziness stand in total contradiction to the calling of being a servant of God. The more we possess the more we can be possessed by the attachments of our godless society. Common sense and a well-balanced personal life ought to be the hallmarks of today's prophet.

The role of prophet frequently calls for a personal price to be paid, usually in the form of a threat to job security. Other times, the price is paid in the form of having to endure professional and personal ridicule, or the guerilla warfare tactics of other department heads sniping away at the programs the chaplain offers for the inmates. Envy and jealousy can motivate a person, who has never built a house, to tear down the house that someone else has built. Professional and personal ridicule, envy and jealousy have always existed in church and state bureaucracies. The chaplain, who serves as a prophet, must know that these ancient forces will always rear their heads to thwart whatever their little minds perceive to be a threat to their secure status quo.

It is vital that the chaplain keep herself free from compromising situations that would have an impact on the truthfulness of her call or her ability to speak at all. If the chaplain finds that she has developed a drug dependency or substance abuse problem, by all means she should seek help immediately to heal that part of her wounded nature. The same would hold true of any other addictive behaviors. If the chaplain does not have these problems in a recovering mode, she will be compromised to the point that her word will have no value and will stand as a sign of ridicule. In that event, the administration winds up with a patsy who can be manipulated any way, any time they want. At that point, both the chaplain and the inmates she serves suffer. Remember, the ancient prophets knew their own personal afflictions and proclaimed them before God. God called them anyway, because they were truthful about their human nature. He helped them rise above it for his sake and the sake of his people.

Being a "good old boy" with the warden is hardly ever appropriate for a chaplain. The chaplain does not work against the warden. But if the chaplain is seen as being too close to, or in the hip pocket of, the warden, the chaplain loses the ability to handle conflict management with the freedom that is necessary for the separation of the essential roles of the church and state. A respectful and cooperative relationship is always to be sought. If the warden needs a pastor, the chaplain should make an appropriate referral to a clergy person in the community in which the warden lives. The chaplain has been hired, first of all, to be the temporary or transitional pastor for the inmates. That is more than a full-time job. The spiritual relationships of all civilian staff should be handled by the chaplain on a temporary basis. Making positive referrals for the civilian staff as soon as possible is to be preferred.

Prophets were not and are not found in civil or religious hierarchies. Neither may the chaplain be.

Of the one who speaks for:

"As the heavens are higher than the earth, so are my ways higher than your ways" (Isaiah 55:9). The chaplain must be constantly searching his mind and heart to discern whose ways he is following. Is he trying to play God, be God, or serve God? Has he succumbed to a twisted logic that he suffers the pangs of insult for the sake of the kingdom, while in reality he induces others to put him down to avoid facing the responsibilities of his actions and teachings? The calling to be a spokesperson for God is more probably genuine when the one called feels a deep reluctance to speak out. As mentioned above, the responsible chaplain must have spiritual consultants and mentors. He must be open to having them advise him that he may be wrong more often than he is right.

All of us are used, had, or abused at one time or another. That happens to all professionals who work for or on behalf of hurting people. Sooner or late this will happen, no matter how smart or skilled we may think we are. But, as a leader said to me one time, after I had been sucked into believing a false story, "Don't quit trying. The inmates need your voice."

To be able to discern whose ways he is following, it is vital that the humble prophet have a sense of humor about his own limitations.

The inmates:

It is an observable fact that some correctional officers and some of the other employees lose sight of their role as rehabilitators and correctors. Some of them have been in positions in their lives where they had to take orders. Now they find themselves having the opportunity to give orders. They take on the conscious or subconscious role of balancing the scales of the pain and hurt they have had to endure in the past. So, now they inflict hurt and pain, mostly psychological, upon the inmates or the employees in other departments.

Added to this phenomenon are those few employees, who believe that the inmates were sent to prison for punishment. They have lost sight of the reality that the inmates were sent to prison as punishment. As a result, these few employees feel it is their proper role to treat the inmates like dogs or dirt. They inflict whatever verbal abuse, and infrequently physical abuse, they feel they want to and whenever they want to. It is obvious that these employees are not the majority. But their very existence can create a mental reign of terror for a lot of inmates.

While the inmates know there is a system of appeal from this sort of abuse, they also know that the abusive employee will very often find a way around the institutional inspector, the major, the deputy warden and the warden. As one lieutenant said to me years ago, after he had been in charge of the rules infraction board for some time, "The most frustrating part of my job is trying to determine who is lying the least — the inmate or the employee."

Added to this burden of the lying employee is the too-frequently accepted dictum, "You can't trust an inmate." The truth is a lot of inmates are not trustworthy. The reality is some are. Knowing the difference can take the wisdom of Solomon. Hence, the chaplain needs to be highly skilled in the psychological sciences and, again, have the constant guidance of spiritual directors.

Definitely, there are times when the inmates need an honest and respected voice. This is especially true at moments of crisis in a prison. It is an observable fact that a chaplain can be a negotiator in an inflammable situation that would otherwise lead to a riot. While few have made the connection, it is an interesting fact that Pennsylvania had its riots after it cut its chaplaincy staff in half. That fact probably was not a major cause of the riots. But the question can be asked, "What would have happened if there had been more religious services staff available; staff who were known for their independent integrity; staff who were known to represent the inmates' needs honestly?"

On behalf of the church to the government:

Seldom is the chaplain assigned to serve on institutional committees that have any real authority in the establishment of philosophy or policy that affect the day-to-day operation of the prison. More often than not, the chaplain's ability to have an impact will rest on his talent to establish trusting relationships on a personal basis. If the chaplain lives out the role of being a pastor, those relationships will develop naturally as the lives of the staff unfold before him. In one institution, the warden's secretary had been given authority to make decisions in areas that normally secretaries are not trained to handle. When I asked to see the warden, she wanted to know the nature of the appointment. When I told her that my reason for seeing the warden was professional, she still insisted that I be more specific. Politely, I told her she did not need to know. While I did get to see the warden, her relationship with me remained cool.

Some months later her mother died. On the night of the visitation at the funeral home, I drove the thirty miles to pay my respects. When I entered the room, the warden's secretary was on the other side, talking to a group of people. When she saw me, she left the others and came directly over. The first thing she said was, "I didn't think you'd come." From that day on, the relationship changed to one of trust and respect.

Through the networking of personal relationships the chaplain will have indirect means to communicate the concerns, beliefs, and practices of the church to the offices and personnel of government. In one-on-one conversations, the chaplain can talk about inmate rights, brutality, overcrowding, cold meals being served to the sick, inadequate medical services, capital punishment and a host of other issues that the church considers vital to the fabric of the integrity of a stable society.

Personal relationships are not always enough to have an impact on the formation of policy. For example, there used to be a practice of permitting inmates to attend the funeral of an immediate family member. Then, after several events of inmates' families helping them escape while attending a funeral, the rules changed. For ten years, some chaplains tried to get the central office staff to reopen the issue of the funeral trip policy. A committee of social workers and psychologists wrote the new rules. Chaplains were not consulted.

Since 1950 the norm for family relationships has become so varied that a number of persons have taken over the usual role of parenting. When chaplains notify inmates of death in their families, it becomes apparent that the present policy of limiting funeral trips to immediate family members is hurting a lot of inmates. For example, while a grandmother was not considered an "immediate family member" in 1950, she may be the only mother today's inmate ever knew. In a system of varied levels of security, it seems that a policy of varied levels of privileges would be in order.

But the reality is, after ten years of trying, nothing has changed. Even when she is not heard, the chaplain, as prophet, must keep speaking to the government as a voice crying in the wilderness. Knowing that people are hurting, she would be untrue to her calling as a chaplain, if she gave up.

As previously mentioned, the chaplain must attend those continuing education conferences sponsored by her denomination or clusters of denominations to stay attuned to the moral, legal and social issues that the churches are addressing in civilian society. Her involvement in a clergy prayer and support group will help her interpret those teachings for the setting in which she serves. In the closed society of the prison, she must constantly be the voice of the church speaking to the government in gentle, yet clear, terms that vengeance, revenge and punishment are not ethically approved ways to lead a person to a rehabilitated life.

In those areas that affect justice, morals, and ethics:

In the biblical sense of the word, justice does not have the connotation of exact equality. Rather, biblical justice refers to a person's receiving what he needs. The American mentality defines justice as fairness. Not infrequently, when people say they have suffered an injustice, they will say, "It's not fair."

The chaplain as prophet works in a legal system, yet represents a religious values system. The perspectives of the two do not always match. Civil legal codes talk about "rights." Religious ethical and moral codes talk about "obligations." The administrator of a 2,500 inmate prison has to be aware of the equality, or "fairness," of the administration of institutional regulations. The chaplain has to be aware of the needs of the individual. In such a large setting balancing fairness with needs will always create a level of tension. The chaplain as prophet must pray continually for the wisdom to know how to walk the fine line between fairness and need.

From the perspective of ministry to the inmates, the chaplain is constantly challenged to preach to them the difference between the civil and religious definitions of justice. Many of the inmates the chaplain will work with are in prison, because they could not accept the truth that life is not fair. It never was. It never will be. In the human order, there will always be an imbalance between what we need and what we see someone else have. Nobody in life gets dealt four aces and a wild card, even when it looks like they do. Nobody gets dealt a perfect hand. Yet the chaplain knows that we all get dealt sufficient grace to carry our individual load.

Most arguments among inmates revolve around the issue of fairness. Most disagreements among employees revolve around the issue of fairness. The challenge for the chaplain as prophet is to speak to both groups in a way that will lead them to let go of what will never be, and to take up a standard that will make community living possible and worthwhile. The person that recognizes that we each have individual needs can look beyond himself to recognize his responsibility to the whole community. The challenge for the chaplain is to lead the inmates and the employees to the vision that their individual talents are meant for the good of the community. When those talents are given in service to the community, the needs of many will be met in the biblical sense of justice. The challenge for the chaplain as prophet is to lead both groups to think in terms of "our" and less in terms of "my."

Many commentators write about the decay of American society. Many point to the church as a reason for the moral decline. Scandals within the leadership of the churches have led people not to listen to what is preached. The greater scandal is that the churches have not preached a moral code in a convincing way that the American people can understand. The chaplain as prophet runs into the same vortex of criticism about moral issues within the institution. The most common problem is that the inmates and the staff expect the chaplain to tell "them" how to behave. And it is always expected that the chaplain is talking about someone other than those people who are immediately present.

The customary ways of right behavior begin with the individual taking responsibility for his own actions. The moral code is not meant to be a mirror that reflects to others that their behavior is embarrassing and "wrong." For example, the warden and the inmate, who liberally sprinkle their speech with gross profanity, are both acting contrary to what is accepted as a right way of behavior. The current custom of saying, "Well, everybody else is doing it," is just as wrong for the employee as it is for the inmate. The chaplain as prophet has to stand as a sign for both groups that a "me"-centered code of morality and ethics will always bring harm and hardship to society in general, and the individual in particular.

As previously noted, one cannot give what one does not have. It the chaplain as prophet is going to be a true prophet, a genuine prophet, her life must stand in public as a witness for a code of living that is moral and ethical. To sign out for administrative leave time to attend a continuing education conference while in reality taking the time to go on vacation, is immoral and unethical. To work on an advanced degree and use the computers and time of the institution to write the dissertation required for the diploma is unethical. The taxpayers are paying for service for the inmates, not for the chaplain to advance himself up the career ladder. To take extended lunch hours is unethical. It is stealing. To become involved in numerous community activi-

ties, while on the time clock of the institution, is just as assur-
edly committing grand theft as the inmate, who is serving time
for robbing a store or home. The chaplain as prophet must never
succumb to the morally-numbing code of, "I'm going to get mine
just like everybody else does."

It may mean personal sacrifice for the chaplain as prophet
to stand out from the ways of behavior that are acceptable to
many in the crowd. Yet, the chaplain will find that there are
many who are waiting for someone to set a better example. They
will follow, if someone has the courage to lead. Among those
things that make a chaplain unique in a prison is the fact that he
is not bucking for promotion. With the primary calling of being
a servant, the chaplain does not have to consider how his actions
and teachings will look and sound when it is time for an annual
review or promotion.

The chaplain as prophet can make the personal sacrifice of
standing for a higher code of morality and ethical behavior because she has nothing to lose. She is going nowhere. She is where
she is called to be. If she doesn't live out her calling, she will
have to answer to a far higher power than the prison administrator could ever dream of possessing. So, when a chaplain finds
herself in a position of being chewed out or threatened with dis-
cipline for what she has said or done contrary to the warden's
code of morality and ethics, she can only smile inside herself at
the futility of an administrator to impose a code of secular behavior that is inane, void and totally without merit, meaning or
relevance. The chaplain as prophet marches to the tune of a different drummer. For the wise administrator, that can be a blessing, a blessing to have someone on the staff who is not afraid to
speak the truth. For the controlling administrator, the chaplain
as prophet will always be an enigma.

The ancient prophets did not want the calling of publicly

preaching the need for repentance and the protection of the weak in society. They knew they would have to pay a personal price for such a ministry. The chaplain as prophet can expect nothing less, as she answers this calling in an unbelieving age.

CHAPTER NINE

THE CHAPLAIN AS POET

The chaplain, by the very role of being a communicator of things seen and unseen, reaches into the depths of her being to pull out and express in unique and imaginative ways the special sensitivity to all the works of creation put before her and in her by God, who created nature and her nature.

One of the greatest theologians of the twentieth century, and possibly one of the greatest in the history of mankind, Teilhard de Chardin, expressed it this way in one of his books. He said that every person, who is called to the ministry of word and sacrament, must be a poet at the core of her being. Teilhard was a man who had special talents that led him to study the very core of the earth. He spent years in deserted parts of China studying rocks. He later wrote, with beautiful expression about the call of each person, the vocation of each person, the destiny of each person to take and lift up creation in a hymn of praise offering it back to the Creator. He was a man who spent years with inanimate objects. Yet, in the middle of Central Park he could stop on a dime, enthralled with the lilting, wafting movements of a butterfly.

The chaplain knows that his main role is that of a communicator, just as the surgeon knows that the centrality of his profession is the cauterizing of flesh in an effort to restore health to the body. But, being true to his profession, and in spite of all the scientific advances brought on and supplemented by technology, the surgeon knows his skills still rely, at their root, on the art of making good judgment calls. He knows that he must be imaginative and creative. He knows that there are things seen and unseen that have to be called upon to restore people to health.

For all the studying she did in the seminary, for all the research she did to pass graduate courses, for all her skills of persuasion by speech, the chaplain knows that there is yet more to communicating. An age-old definition of prayer is: the lifting of the mind and heart to God.

Many chaplains were trained in the skills of lifting the mind to God. Many chaplains are skilled in communicating and understanding the written word of God in the revealed writings of the faith. Many chaplains can speak for hours on the theories and theologies presented by Augustine, Aquinas, Luther, Calvin, Wesley, Newman, Kirkegaard, Rahner and Merton. Many chaplains can wax eloquently about things seen and unseen.

Other chaplains come from organizational backgrounds that emphasize emotions more than the mind in worship or prayer. These groups engage the heart with spontaneous expressions of joy with outbursts of "Amen!" and "Alleluia!" and "Right on!" and "Say it again, brother!" Other groups express the levels of joy in the rhymes of speech or the swaying of bodies, or swooning in the front of the sanctuary, or in the clapping of hands, or in a modified movement of dance. Having done all or some of these things, they are convinced that they have engaged the mind and the heart in prayer. To a degree that may be true. But it is not all there is to the picture of being a minister of the word and sacrament from the perspective of poetry, from the perspective of the art and the artist.

How is the chaplain a communicator of things unseen? Perhaps another way to phrase it is in the words of Scripture: "They have eyes, but do not see; they have ears, but do not hear" (Jeremiah 5:21). The chaplain, as a person who has had general exposure to many areas of knowledge, knows that ninety percent of all communication is body language, not verbal expression, not unending verbiage.

The chaplain knows the many places in the revealed writings that can be summarized with this phrase, "Be still and know that I am God" (Psalm 46:10). The chaplain knows that the volume of the singing is not necessarily directly related to better singing. She knows that shouting joyfully to the Lord is not the only way to express joy as an individual or as a community. She knows that the flow of a quiet tear can be the release of many years of yearning to praise God in a way that words cannot express, when our words fall short. She knows that the quiet flow of a tear can be the expression of the moment of acknowledging responsibility for one's actions and the acceptance of God's forgiveness and the forgiveness of self, which is immeasurably harder to achieve. She knows that the quiet flow of a tear can be the expression of the release of pent-up anger and frustration that has blocked the grip of grace for that soul for ages.

There once was a warden who, when told about the many inmates who shed tears of joy and anger and forgiveness in a chaplain's office, laughed. He laughed with a nod of knowing smugness that said, without words, "That's what you expect of a wimpish person; wimpish things takes place in his office. God! Why do we pay for such silliness?" That warden had carried such a burden of anger in his own private life for so many years that he couldn't see the beauty of life-giving joy and forgiving sorrow.

The warden couldn't understand that the internal change that was taking place in the lives of the inmates was the fundamental purpose for which his prison existed. He didn't know how to approach life. He was afraid of the freedom of life. He didn't know that he was called by the Creator of all things to let go of the bondage of anger and smugness. He didn't know that he was called, that his purpose in life was to lift up his body and mind and soul in joyful praise to his Creator. He was like the former national chairman of the Republican Party, who, when faced with brain cancer, apologized to all those he hurt with his arrogant, smug self-righteousness, saying, "I missed the purpose of life." Somewhere the warden and the national chairman needed the poetic ministering of a skilled chaplain.

Prison life is full of noise. When Jesus needed to refresh his spiritual energies, he went off into a deserted place for a long period of time. Those inmates, who are sensitive to God's call to them, crave, more than anything, a place of silence. The American prison system is caught up in the ugly American philosophy of utilitarianism: "If it isn't functional and useful all the time, it doesn't need to exist." We erect buildings for maximum use, not maximum esthetics. We build cars for maximum efficiency, not maximum beauty. Prisons are built for programs and activities. The buildings have to have a function that can be used by groups for "doing" something productive.

Sensitive line officers know that the inmates need a quiet place, a quiet space. Legislators and administrators build Religious Services Centers that can be used for AA and NA meetings and music association practice sessions and college courses and orientation sessions. God forbid that we should have a quiet place, where people can get in touch with themselves; where people can be still and hear the word of rehabilitation God has for them.

The saddest aspect of all this cacophony and programming is that some chaplains go right along with it. They get sucked into the American ethic of group usefulness. When they conduct a worship service or invite in an outside faith group, many of them have to have the latest and loudest sound equipment, equipment sufficient to peel the paint off the walls of Carnegie Hall with all the vibrations. Much of the service is spent in earsplitting singing. The rest is spent in preaching that is hallmarked by its shouting. Where is the quiet? Where is the stillness? Where, in the course of scheduling all sorts of activities, is the scheduling of time in the overall program for quiet and individual meditation and reflection and prayer? Where is the time to "Be still and know that I am God"? The chaplain as poet must be sensitive to this powerful life-changing form of communication.

Along with being a teacher of the Bible, the Ta'lim or the Torah, perhaps the chaplain should be the leader and convener of regular sessions of meditation.

During a retreat presented in our main worship hall a few years ago, the opening speaker said to the eighty inmates gathered in the room, "For the next hour we're going to meditate." At that time, I had worked in prisons for twelve years. This retreat speaker was presenting his first talk ever in a prison setting. So I, in my smugness, said to myself, "Sure, bud. You think you're going to get these guys to sit still for one hour. You've got an education coming!" Well, for the next hour I was the one who received an education. You couldn't hear a belch or a burp or a cough out of that crowd. The leader had them open the windows and listen to the wind, listen to the leaves, listen to the birds, listen to creation. And they listened as though they had never heard before. They listened to the creation of their God and imagined what it must have been like for Adam to walk in the cool of the garden with God. They imagined what a depth of love, what a depth of trust there was that didn't need to be expressed with words; that couldn't be expressed with words.

Lusty singing on Sunday is good. But it is not all that there is to worship. The chaplain as poet, who neglects to balance the harmonic resonances in community with the stillness of nature, is neglecting his calling, his job.

Years ago, while managing the operations of a number of cemeteries for my denomination, I came up with the idea of having a logo that would be used by all the cemeteries in our region. I hoped that all of our people would recognize the logo, whenever they would be visiting our cemeteries. They would know our vehicles and our employees and would identify our advertising immediately, when they would see the logo. The consultant we hired for the job asked what we were trying to convey by the logo. He asked what we wanted people to feel, when they saw it. We told him we wanted to convey a sense of peace, strength, calm and assurance. He responded, "Then your dominant colors should be blue and green." Blue and green. Think of it. What two colors fill our world more than any other — blue and green! The Creator knew what he was doing when He gave us the colors of peace, strength, calm and assurance.

When people look at a brilliant sunset, they have two impulses. One is to find someone to share it with. The other, after gazing at the gold, yellow, amber, brilliant blue, soft purple, stunning red and burnt orange, is to say from the depths of the soul, "Thank you, God, for letting me see such a beautiful sight."

Some denominations take positions about the decorating of their churches on the basis of what they have seen as excesses in other denominations. In contrast to the excesses, they build worship centers that are stark and barren. Yet, at second sight that is really not the case. For, if you looked closely, you will note the brilliant red carpet, or the royal blue padding of the pews, or the stunning white and purple of the choir robes. Colors speak to people. God created the colors. When man destroys or abuses the earth, he creates brown and black. The deserts and burned-out cities created by man create colors that speak of desolation and depression. Of what do these colors in our prisons and our prison worship centers speak? Have we noticed?

When I first arrived at my second prison assignment, I noticed that the buildings were surrounded by trees. The open spaces also had an abundance of trees. At that time, such landscaping was unlike any other prison I had ever seen. Later that day when I met with the warden, I said, "No matter what you do with this old place, no matter whether you tear it down or add, please don't remove a tree." He smiled a soft, knowing smile that said, without saying, "You bet I won't." Then I noticed a Holy Spirit pin in his lapel. He knew that all of creation awaits the coming of the Lord. He knew that trees and color speak a language of God; a language of life the inmates need to hear.

Most of the men, who come to prison, come from a socioeconomic background where brick and clapboard and cement and dust are the common sights in the neighborhood. Rare is it that a real manicured lawn or garden or flower bed is seen. Then, when they do see such a thing, it is not really seen because it is not expected. For example, in 1964, I saw a young man carrying his radio. He held it next to his ear. His head was bowed down as he walked. He was walking through Franklin Park in Columbus. It was early May. He was walking past flowering trees, yellow daffodils, red tulips, purple hyacinths, white alyssum and blue ageratums. Robins and tanagers were singing. He had eyes, but did not see. He had ears, but did not hear. His culture and his church had not taught him to expect to see or hear God in such beauty. The tragedy is he was less of a person because of it.

At the Religious Services Centers, where I have worked, we have had the most beautiful flower displays within the compound. In fact, the Religious Services Center was the first place to develop flower beds with design, color and artistry in mind. Our sidewalks were lined with flowers. Our trees and our building were surrounded by flowers. They were planted with a purpose and a pattern that was intended to be pleasing to the eye. In our preaching, we called attention to the flowers as gifts of God's creation. We invited the men to smell the fragrances that are naturally pleasing. Men would cut across our lawn, instead of using our sidewalk. Employees as well would cut across our lawn, in spite of the signs that told them not to do so. But none of them, inmates and employees alike, would step on or pick a flower. The inmates would destroy all other state property to the tune of thousands of dollars. But they would not destroy a flower. As he was going home, one man said to me, "Thank you for exposing me to the beauty God has given us in this life through flowers. I never noticed a flower in my thirty-seven years, until I came here. Thank you for opening my eyes." He spoke of beauty and life. When you see and experience it, really see and experience it, you can't destroy it.

Where else in a prison is a man going to get this opportunity to have his senses and his heart elevated to a language of God that is spoken so eloquently in nature? As communicator and poet, the chaplain must be sensitive to what a person yearns for from the depth of his being.

We spent about three hundred dollars a year when we decorated our chapel for Christmas. When the men came into the chapel for the first time to see our decorations, it was for the Christmas Eve ecumenical candlelight service. The velvet green of the trees, the brilliant red and white and pink of poinsettias, the soft flicker of candles in the windows — all these created an environment. In that environment each year, some of the men would spontaneously respond by falling to their knees in quiet, reverential prayer. Color speaks to the heart a language of prayer like no other language.

Sometime in our life we have been exposed to the experience that when we whisper, others around us will automatically whisper or speak softly too. When people walk into a room, where soft background music is being played, they tend to speak less. When people come into a worship room, where others are speaking at random, it is nearly impossible to prepare the mind and heart for the prayer service that is to begin in just a few minutes. Sound can prepare the mood and the mind for the theme of the prayer service.

Just as a violin can be played in various ways to express joy, excitement, sorrow, pensiveness, anguish, somber meditation, and flirtatiousness, so can music in worship be used for many expressions. All sorts of moods, with all sorts of sounds, from all sorts of instruments can be skillfully, artfully, and imaginatively presented to lift the heart and mind in prayer. To play and sing the same old prison music, week after week, is to pander to lower tastes and deprive the men of the experience of lifting the soul to God in a healthy variety of forms and volumes. One way to expose the inmates to a new style of music is to play that new form through the sound system as the inmates are gathering for worship. After several weeks of such background preparation, the Sunday that the new music is used in the worship service, it will not seem as startling as when it was heard for the first time. In this mode of gradual preparation, the music can be heard for what it was intended, an expression of prayer.

One Sunday at the seminary, we sang Psalm 150 to the accompaniment of music written by a modern composer. The music was played with trumpets, violins, organ, piano, drums and tambourines. When the pastors in the city near the seminary were told about the use of drums, violins and tambourines at worship, they raised a howl of protest to the president of the seminary. In response he invited them to join us for worship the following Saturday. At that time, we again played and sang the new version of Psalm 150. After that worship, every single pastor said he enjoyed the new musical form. Newness does not mean awfulness. Newness means a challenge to stretch our appreciation of what God could be telling us through the talents of others.

There are many modern composers who feel that they must express or reflect the society in which they live. So they use atonal expressions and twelve tonal expressions, dissonance and cacophony, and discordant and strident themes. For many people, their music is hard to listen to and appreciate. It may be that these composers are doing society a service by truly expressing and reflecting the resonances of a sinful and materialistic world gone astray from its roots and ultimate meaning. Yet, studies tell us that most people know that they are sinful and wounded in their nature. What most people need is a musical form that leads them to the courage and joy of acknowledging their true worth as children of God. For the lifting of the spirit in prayer, we have the beautiful and the harmonious and expressive deposits of music left to us through Gregorian Chant, Handel and Haydn, Mozart and Brahms, Beethoven and Mahler, and many, many others. The chaplain as poet must be attuned to sound, all sorts of sound, and all cultural expressions of sound. She must be aware of all the subtle and not so subtle effects sound can have on the heart that is attempting to lift itself to union with God.

The Bible is replete with the imagery of light: "You are the light of the world" (Matthew 5:14) and "Let your light shine before men... in order that they may give glory to your Father in heaven" (Matthew 5:16). The chaplain as poet must be aware of the effects of light upon the people at the time of public prayer and when they are in private prayer.

Recent studies from science have shown that light fights depression. People, who are prone to depression in the winter can fight it off by sitting under certain kinds of light for short periods of time each day. Light affects the mind. It can also affect the heart at prayer. At a funeral service a few years ago, all the lights but one were dimmed during the time of the reception of communion. One soft light was focused on the wall behind the communion table. While the Twenty-Third Psalm was sung a capella, slides were projected on that circle of light, slides that depicted scenes from the Twenty-Third Psalm. The totality of light and darkness, shadow and color created a prayerful, calm and moving moment for reflection.

While giving a talk during a retreat, a talk on the theme of "You are the light of the world," the retreat master asked for all the lights in the room to be turned out. Then, with the flick of a match, he lit one candle. He continued to hold that candle for the rest of his talk. Near the end of his talk he was saying what the world would be like without the Light of Christ. Then, when he finished his talk, he blew out the candle, plunging the room into darkness. The retreatants got the message.

During our Christmas Eve service, before the last song, the lights are turned out except for the lights on the Christmas trees, the candles at the altar, and the candles in the windows. Then each inmate is given a candle to hold as well. The soft glow on each man's face, and the diffusion of that soft light throughout the hall as they sing "Silent Night" is a sight and sound to behold. You can't help but wonder if the experience is in some way similar to what the shepherds heard in that soft light of the stars shining over the fields on the first Christmas. During the second verse of the song, we encourage the men to lift high their candles. Then the glow that made the faces shine now becomes rays that descend on all. The symbolism of each person's faith shared with all the others, creating a brilliant beauty as a gift for the creator, is not missed by those present.

Shadow and darkness, brilliance and subtle shade — all forms of light, when used creatively, and imaginatively, can support and attract the attention of the heart to pray.

The Bible says that man was created a little less than the angels (Psalm 8:5; Hebrews 2:7). What a magnificent concept! That of all of this creation, man is the pinnacle. However, modern man seems to be out of harmony with what he was created to be. Modern man seems to be out of tune with nature. The tall buildings he erected from the 1960's through the 1980's were square and flat, cold and ugly, depressing to the human spirit. In more recent years, architects have retrofitted some of these high-rises with pitched roofs, so that they can be more pleasing to the eye and elevate man's spirit. What the architects missed before the 1990's was that God had already designed nature in a way to lift the spirit of mankind. For example, if you look at nature and the human being, you do not see straight lines. You do not see colors and shapes that stand in gaudy contrast. You see warmth and softness in curves and subtlety. You see shape and color that blend and complement. The Creator knew what He was doing.

When you talk to people who are seated in straight rows of chairs, you get far less response from them than when you speak to them while they are seated in a semi-circle. Nature abhors straight lines. The shapes of nature speak to the heart of warmth and majestic beauty. They speak of the love of God for man by creating a welcome supportive environment.

The chaplain as poet must be aware of the shape of her worship center. Is it inviting? Does it speak a language to the heart that says God is here in this community at prayer?

The chaplain as poet also must be aware of the shape of man. He must be able to express in words the beauty that God has created in man. He must be able to speak about a beauty in humankind that is not humanistic, but a beauty that is put there by God to reflect the magnificent worth of each person.

Our men and women need to be told convincingly that there is a difference between generating life and creating life. They must be told what a splendid difference there is between the two. They need to be encouraged to visit museums and art galleries to see how the souls of others have striven to reflect the beauty of creation in man, a reflection that speaks of God's love. They need to see the beauty that can exist when a man refuses to be used by drugs. They need to see the beauty that can exist when a woman refuses to be used as a sex object, or to be abused by alcohol. They need to see the beauty that can exist, when a man refuses to succumb to greed.

Our inmates need to see human lives as they are respected and captured by the great artists and sculptors. They need to hear that it is okay to love themselves; to love all of our physical selves, because that is precisely what God made. They need to see the fantastic beauty of a simple smile. God gave each of us a smile that no artist or sculptor can duplicate, as much as they may try. The artist strives to capture the human spirit; but the depictions of the artist are mere reflections of what God has created in the flesh.

The chaplain as poet must be able to communicate to her congregation not only the great gift of the mind of man, but the magnificence of the glorious shape of the human being. As long as we are trapped in the materialistic imagery of what a beautiful person is supposed to be, to that degree are we trapped in our ability to give praise to God for the physical and spiritual uniqueness of the individual human person.

The notion that a person can do what he wants with his body also must be fought with the perspective of a poet who proclaims that a person does not come into this world on his own and does not leave this world on his own. The notion that a person can do what he wants with his body must be answered from the perspective of St. Paul, who speaks eloquently of the gifts that have been given to each person from God (1 Corinthians 12). It is almost a cliche today to say that what our inmates need is the development of self-esteem. The chaplain as poet should be preaching and teaching in such a way that an increase in self-esteem is a natural and supernatural result.

In addition to those churches that design their worship centers in a plain fashion based upon their young theological traditions, the older churches of European ancestry also tired of their inherited signs and symbols in the 1960's. In some artistic circles, it became chic to paint worship centers in stark white. The expression of the day was for clerics to discard professional clothing or symbols. Churches were designed to look like banks or auditoriums. Steeples and crosses were passe. While the mood and move was to throw out the excesses of those who *played* church rather than *being* church, one excess was replaced with another — the excess of no signs and no symbols.

In the history of all the cultures of humankind, two things stand out as constants. There were always jails and altars. There is something deep within the heart of humankind that recognizes that we are not our own creation. There is something deep within the heart of humankind that recognizes that we fail to give honor and glory to God and God's creation.

As the older, more "sophisticated" churches threw out signs and symbols from the past, it often happened that the new store-front, grassroots churches took them up. Sometimes they literally bought them from the mainline churches. Self-anointed and self-appointed ministers began wearing Roman collars. Women in these congregations took to using as a formal and public title the appellation "Sister." When once it was only the Catholic churches that had crosses on top of the steeples, the new churches began to put crosses all over the place — on signs in front of the church, on the front of the church, in the vestibule, and in the sanctuary. While this movement is not universal to the new American churches, there has been a definite swing back to the use of signs and symbols that says that this is a place or a person dedicated to God for service to the whole community.

There is something in the heart of humankind that tells us that we need signs and symbols to remind us of our purpose in life. It is not just the psychological reaction of a person under threat of loss of life in a foxhole wanting to pray. The person in prison and the person in civilian society have both known times in their lives when they feel empty. They both sense an uprootedness. Both search for something; some sign of normalcy and continuity to hang onto. They both need some sign of strength and assurance that the whole world has not turned upside down. For a while, both of them may turn to religious signs and symbols as a sort of Linus blanket. But, after the initial shock of what may be called crisis moments, both the inmate and the civilian want and use signs and symbols as guideposts. They use them as reminders of their calling to live a life in union with the Creator. They use them in much the same way they use pictures to remind them of their loved ones who are not physically present at the moment.

The chaplain as poet needs to use signs and symbols that speak of strong faith. The chaplain as poet needs to use signs and symbols that say religion is unlike all the ordinary, soul-degrading routines of prison life. Signs and symbols need to tell the inmates that they and their place of worship are special. The chaplain as poet needs to use signs and symbols that tell the inmates that life is to be exalted; that they are a people called to visibly serve the non-faith community; that they are visibly trying to live out their lives in witness to the God who has called them to be special, persons loved by the Beloved.

One Good Friday the two of us chaplains held an ecumenical service for the inmates. We placed a rugged cross in the chancel. The cross was made from trees that had just been hewn the day before. During the service, we gave thirty inmates three-by-five cards with messages on them to be read from the pews in the congregation. Each message described a particular sin of mankind. Each message ended with the phrase, "forgive us for nailing you to the cross with our sins." After reading the card, each man would come forward and nail the card to the cross. The thud of the hammer on the nail, as the card was posted on the cross, echoed in the stillness through the church. The poignant sound spoke a message to the heart that no sermon could preach.

The Bible speaks of lifting up our prayers like incense before God (Psalm 141:2). Just because one church uses incense doesn't mean that other churches can't use the same symbol. Some churches baptize by immersion in water; some by pouring water; others by sprinkling water. Water is common to all faiths as a sign and symbol and reality of cleansing and purification. A washing of the feet ceremony is appropriate for Christians during Holy Week, but it does not have to be limited to that week only. The chaplain as poet needs to feel free to express the commonality of signs and symbols used by other denominations and other faiths.

During our Ash Wednesday service, each inmate is invited to write on a small piece of paper the acts of self-denial and the acts of good works he plans to do during the Lenten season. Those folded and unsigned slips of paper are then put in a collection basket and placed on the table in front of the altar at each worship service during Lent. These slips of paper become a visible reminder of what we individually, and as a community, have dedicated ourselves to doing in faith. During our Easter service, those papers are burned, and the fire is used to light the Paschal candle. This part of our Easter service symbolizes that Christ destroys sins, wipes them away and becomes the Light of the World for us. We, civilians and inmates, come to realize that this light can be readily shared through our acts of self-denial and charity.

While giving a talk about sin to a group of inmates on retreat, the speaker started by lighting a stick of incense. He gave no explanation for his action. During his talk, the incense kept burning. It became more and more powdery ash. As the incense burned out, the speaker concluded his talk with this final comment, "When our sins are confronted by God's mercy, they become like these ashes." Then he blew the ashes away.

The chaplain as poet needs to be constantly reaching back into the history of how other Christians expressed their faiths. She needs to be open to how other groups today are expressing their faiths. She needs to take these signs and symbols and use the ones that speak to her congregation, to their hearts at prayer.

Light and color. Sound and shape. Sign and symbol. The chaplain might know the great works of literature. He should know them. As poet he should know how other people have struggled to express faith and the meaning of life. He should have read books by Malcolm X and Frederick Douglass, by Hawthorne and Shakespeare, by Charlotte Bronte and Emily Dickinson, by Marcus Garvey and Martin Luther King, by Koestler and Camus. He should be facile and current with great literature, with great works of the mind. He should be able to use them fluently and relevantly that the inmates may know the struggles and triumphs of people of faith throughout the ages and across cultures. He should be able to relate the great works of literature in such a way that the inmates may learn the messages of life that are lived, and have been lived, by people who have read the scriptures, and by those who have rejected them.

If the chaplain leaves out the language of the heart — the language of light and color, the language of sound and shape, the language of sign and symbol, the language of prose, poetry and philosophy — she will be as the tin man in "The Wizard of Oz," an empty shell.

Chapter Ten

THE CHAPLAIN AS
VOLUNTEER COORDINATOR

If by some first-class miracle the chaplaincy should be funded and staffed at the levels recommended by the federal government, it would still fall upon the role of the chaplain to recruit, train and coordinate volunteers for the needs of the programs of the Religious Services Center, both inside and outside the prison.

There are some within the chaplaincy who say that the chaplain should be more than a glorified coordinator of volunteer services. Their objection is that this is what some chaplains have become at some prisons. At the prisons where I have worked, we have never had enough volunteers. In a recent year, we had 1,539 visits by volunteers. Every one of them was providing some immediate or direct extension of pastoral care to one of our eight faith groups. These services they provided were in addition to the pastoral care we chaplains supplied. Until we reach Utopia where each inmate would have a personal, trained, well-educated and mature spiritual mentor as a guide for basic tenets of religious belief, we will never have enough religious volunteers.

In addition to immediate and direct services to the inmates,

121

we need a host of well-trained volunteers to assist with all the office and management responsibilities that are needed to keep the operations going from behind the scenes.

Finally, there is a need for hundreds of volunteers to be active outside the prison. They provide material, social, medical, employment and spiritual support for inmates who have been released from prison. In addition, when our limited budget is not enough, these people raise funds for, or collect, the wide variety of supplies and furnishings needed to maintain all the religious worship services and religious education classes inside the institution.

Our job description recently allowed for the chaplain to spend up to ten percent of his time providing public relations in the community on behalf of the prison. However, the fact of the matter is we chaplains were too busy providing direct pastoral care to be able to do public relations work on "company time." What actually happened was that we arranged talks, radio programs and television shows for a variety of church and service organizations for after hours and on our days off.

As previously mentioned, most administrators do not realize that the chaplains spend an average of four hours per week on professional reading and sermon preparation at home. This reading and preparation work is directly related to work in the prison. In addition to this, it is not unusual for the chaplain to spend several more hours per week answering phone calls at home from volunteers, former inmates, community service organizations, and family and friends of inmates. There are some chaplains, who have their phone numbers unlisted, so that they will not be bothered by some of these sources. However, it is my opinion that a pastor would be derelict in duty to make himself unavailable to the individuals and groups that are directly involved in, or related to, the prison ministry he has agreed to serve.

I know that this opinion is not well-received by some chaplains. I know that it can be inconvenient to be so available. However, the question that comes to mind repeatedly is, "What did you get ordained to be?" Certainly, the call to be of service in religious ministry was not a call to convenience or personal gratification. Certainly, the Christian chaplain, familiar with Luke 1:35-39, would find grounding for his personal life of a balanced rhythm of engagement and rest in ministry.

When it comes to giving talks to religious groups and community organizations some years are busier than others. During the first two years of ministry at the prison where I recently served, twenty-six presentations were made each year. In the last eight years, that number leveled off to an average of ten talks per year. The size of the groups varied from as small as ten to unknown hundreds and thousands when we spoke over the radio or television. Whatever the size of the group and whether we were enlisting volunteer or material support, the number one reason for the presentation was to request prayer support. Only once did a community pastor refuse to offer prayer support. His community had a long way to go, I should think, before it could be said that they were a part of the Body of Christ.

Another avenue for recruiting volunteers and support was through newsletters, newspapers and the public relations offices of established faith groups. Through these avenues we averaged one story per month getting the word out to church people and to the public at large about our prison ministry. We wrote articles and announcements for church bulletins, newsletters, newspapers and a national magazine.

We made two half-hour television shows that were broadcast over local religious facilities in our area in recent years. At another prison in the 1970's, we were guests on a religious talk show on television once every three months. Over the years, the chaplains I have worked with and I have been part of radio talk shows in Cincinnati, Dayton, Springfield, Columbus and Cleveland.

The avenues for soliciting help and getting the word out about ministries in a prison are as broad as the communication channels are available in the area where the prison is located. With imagination and help from professionals in public relations work, those avenues of communication can be statewide and nationwide.

It takes a lot of work to build a team of almost four hundred volunteers. It takes a lot of work after "regular business hours" to keep such a team together, to train new volunteers and to keep their services growing. But, without them, our services to the inmates would be less than half what it is at the present time.

For example, on a given Saturday I may have eight volunteers, trained for special tasks, working with me during my eight hour day. During that time we have a devotional prayer service, a Mass, two music practices, a Ta'lim session, a Jehovah's Witness worship group, a hospital visitation team and a solitary confinement visitation team. At the same time, we are registering men for various faith groups, teaching an R.C.I.A. class, and giving out Bibles, Korans, greeting cards, rosaries, crosses and crucifixes. In the midst of all this, it is not unusual to receive two to four calls from family members of inmates telling us that a relative has died or is in the hospital in critical condition.

Also, on Saturday, there is usually a line of inmates who want to see me about personal problems that can range from thoughts of suicide, to marital problems, to threats being made on their lives by other inmates, to spiritual guidance with their personal prayer life, to problems of religious persecution from other inmates and staff, to being worried because they have had no mail from home in a month. All of the services we provide on a Saturday are legitimate pastoral care programs. It is not unusual for us to provide direct and indirect service to between three and four hundred inmates on a Saturday. The simple fact of the matter is that I, as one person, could in no way provide all these services for all these people in one day. Without the team of well-trained volunteers, I might be able to see fifty of those men in a direct service way. By using a team of volunteers, our ministry at the Religious Services Center is multiplied by six to eight times. The reason for our not doing even more work and providing even more services and programs at this time is that we do not have the rooms available for more volunteers to join us in providing those individual and group services.

While nearly four hundred people volunteer their services within the prison, not all of those who are interested in prison ministry are suited to working directly with inmates. Some of those not interested in working personally inside the prison support our ministry on the outside. There are those who make cash donations to our tax-exempt incorporated volunteer organization. There are those who work from their homes, by providing management of the cash assets of our volunteer organization. Some provide secretarial assistance by writing "thank you" notes to the donors that support the volunteer activities. Other volunteers provide their services by telephoning the members of the group to remind them of group meetings.

Another avenue of great assistance from our volunteers is the help to write grants to fund programs the state is not likely to provide. Our organization had five grants given to us through such help. Other volunteers help with writing newsletters and mailing them to church groups in our area. Some volunteers provide support by contacting the media and arranging for publicity for our projects. Other volunteers provide assistance by talking to their state representatives and senators and other elected officials. There are also volunteers who represent us chaplains at meetings of other volunteer groups, who are working in areas of peace and justice at the local, state, and regional church levels. They present workshops and provide displays of our literature and pictures of our work. At other times, they serve as panel members at conferences and adult education programs.

Those who wish to be of more support to our needs inside the prison, and yet do not have the time or inclination to come inside, offer their services in still other ways. One group collects books and magazines from churches and individuals all over the metropolitan area. They are trained by us to sort out those kinds of literature that are unacceptable according to security standards (provided by the prison administration) and moral standards (provided by the chaplains). Then they box the materials and deliver them to us once a month. The chaplains then give the materials a final review before distributing them to the dorms and hospital wards and the nursing home.

Still other volunteers coordinate the purchase of Christmas items that are given through the chaplains to the inmates at Christmas time. These volunteers arrange for the packaging of the items and the delivery of the decorated bags to the individual dorms. One volunteer coordinates the purchasing. Eight volunteers arrange the items for assembly. Another eighty volunteers provide the delivery and distribution. With the five thousand dollars donated to us from individuals, churches and groups, we are able to shop wholesale and purchase items that would retail for nine thousand dollars. Two hundred and twenty-three contributors made the project possible in 1997. Thus, this one project that essentially takes place outside the prison involves three hundred and twenty people over a period of three months. Their numbers are not included in the previously mentioned

1,539 visits of volunteers, who come to work inside the prison.

There are yet other volunteers, who arrange transportation for family members to come to visit relatives at the prison. Some volunteers come to the prison to provide transportation for recently-released inmates to get home. Still others assist recently-released inmates to find jobs and housing, get registered with local law enforcement agencies, and obtain temporary driver's licenses.

Some volunteers will take the newly-released inmate to his first AA or NA meeting, or will go with him to church on Sunday to introduce him to the pastor and to be with him for the initial few worship services in those crucial first weeks. Other volunteers assist the newly-released inmate with obtaining a wardrobe and work clothes and furnishings for an apartment. Some will provide temporary transportation to get the man to and from his job.

Other volunteers will help the newly-released inmate get acquainted with medical personnel in the area. Some have helped get the newly-released inmate registered in college. A few have even paid for the first quarter of college education. Others give of their time and energies to provide social support by taking the newly-released inmate shopping with them, or taking them along on a family picnic, or taking them to various community festivals, or for walks in the metropolitan parks, or to museums, or to the zoo, or to arrange a birthday party for them, and to send them Christmas gifts, even gifts to the former inmate's children.

Another avenue of assistance from volunteers is the help they give us in the purchase of typewriters and computers, chairs and tables, copy machines and hymnals, liturgical vestments, altars and a pulpit, carpets and bookshelves, file cabinets and televisions, VCRs and slide projectors, overhead projectors and couches, end tables and lamps, clocks, coffee urns and coffee, cups and Kleenex supplies, pictures and Christmas decorations, kneelers and communion tables, sacred vessels of all varieties and religious affiliations, flowers for Easter and Christmas, flowers to grow in our yard and in the hospital courtyard, foods for religious festivals — foods that are required and are not stocked by the state, birthday cakes for the Religious Services Center staff, Bibles, video tapes and audio cassettes. Over the last ten years, we have had tons of equipment donated, collected or paid for by volunteers. Most of this has come from people who have never, and will never, come inside the prison to provide direct assistance to the inmates.

Who are all these volunteers, and where do they come from? The women and men, who assist us inside the prison and outside the prison, range in age from their middle twenties to nearly eighty years old. Aside from the elderly who are retired, almost all the other volunteers have full-time jobs and still find time to help us. Most are employees, some from small businesses and some from nationally-recognized corporations. Others are owners of their own businesses, and some are corporate officers of large businesses. Still others represent a variety of professions, including doctors, lawyers, teachers, engineers, architects, pastors, nuns, scientists and accountants. All are affiliated with a faith group and have the authorization of their clergy person to be representing their faith communities as they assist us in pastoral ministry.

For all our volunteers, we have compiled a set of papers describing who we are and what we do. Another part of the packet of papers tells them about what their relationship should be with the inmates. The papers tell them about state rules and regulations; about contraband and weapons; about drugs and appropriate communications; and about suitable clothing. They are required to sign a form that says they have read and agree to abide by prison regulations. They are provided training through our training officer.

Those volunteers who are going to work with us on a regular basis on the inside of the prison must be willing to work under the supervision of a full-time or contract chaplain. They must work under our direct supervision for six months before they are given a volunteer's identification badge that permits entry without an escort into the Religious Services Center or other areas of authorized ministry. They must be willing to work under supervision at all times and submit written reports of their activities when necessary.

During their six months' training, the regular volunteers are asked to work with us in a variety of settings. During this time, we introduce them to the security staff and inmates. Time is set aside for them to ask questions, and for us to explain to them what it is that we are doing, why we do it, and how we do it. We also review with them some of the personality traits of the inmates. Finally, we review the basic do's and don't's of security, for the area in which they will work.

After eight weeks of the training program, we gradually let them take the lead in that area of service they will be providing. During this phase, we follow them and observe them to see whether they have picked up the basics of what is necessary to be an asset to us and to the inmates. Over the years, our security staff became acquainted with our training modes. They were very cooperative in working with the new volunteers, assisting in training them and guiding them. The shift captains and lieutenants were especially helpful in this capacity.

Many times volunteers do not know where and how they can best contribute their time, energy and talents. For the vast majority of our volunteers, their coming to help us is the first time they have ever been in a prison, and the first time they have ever spoken to or worked with an inmate. In these cases, we ask the volunteers to come visit us on several different days and evenings of the week to see what varieties of ministries there are in an active Religious Services Center. During this time, we explain to the inmates and security personnel that these people are with us just to observe and to discern what they may do to help us. Usually they will spot two or three areas of ministry they would like to try. Through a further period of discernment with the volunteer, we usually arrive at a mutually-agreed-upon task with which the volunteer is comfortable. Occasionally a volunteer finds he or she is not really able to handle the area of ministry that first appealed to them. Again, through periods of prayerful discernment and consultation with the chaplain, they usually find where the best area of their talents lie.

Not all who volunteer to work with us inside or outside the prison are suited to prison ministry. On their own, some come to recognize that they are not able to relate to the types of ministry we need. Some feel they do not have the personality to relate to the inmates. After a period of time, they come to recognize that their giftedness to the faith community lies in another area.

Seldom do we have a volunteer leave us in sheer frustration that the task is too much for them. Most often those volunteers who cease working with us do so because of family conflicts — e.g., someone is sick at home — not because their family members do not want them working at the prison. Sometimes they have to leave us because they or their spouses are transferred to a new job in another city. Other times, career developments in their primary job causes a change in their work hours. Also, there are times when the limitations imposed by advancing age cause them to decide that they can no longer be of help.

It just becomes too much for them physically. In every one of these scenarios, when the volunteer leaves us, we and the inmates feel as though we have lost a family member. The mutuality of support between volunteers, inmates and chaplains strengthens the faith walk of all of us, regardless of denomination or faith affiliation.

In a less positive vein, the experience of working with volunteers does include those who seem driven by another source to be an authority unto themselves. We have had volunteers who come to the volunteers' meetings on the outside, and within two meetings tell the veteran volunteers what is wrong with the organization, and how the whole organization should be restructured. The veteran volunteers have had to have the grace of character and internal strength to tell the "reformer" that the new "direction" is not workable.

We have also had those volunteers who come inside the prison feeling that they answer to a "higher authority." They presume they do not have to follow our rules, rules established to provide for safety and security for volunteers, employees and inmates. One man told us he was not responsible for extending his prayer group meeting beyond the time allotted. He said he was late in releasing the men to return to their dorms because the Holy Spirit was leading him in prayer at that time. The chaplain told the volunteer that the Holy Spirit knows how to tell time. The volunteer was not invited back.

Another volunteer repeatedly refused to follow our guidelines in ministering to the sick, attempting to bring in items the inmates were not permitted to have, or dressing in clothes we have said volunteers should not wear, or forgetting to bring positive identification, or attempting to bring another volunteer who was not trained or approved for our work. When he was confronted with his constant attempts to ignore our guidelines, he responded that he had to follow the higher authority of the Holy Spirit. The chaplain told him the higher authority of the Holy Spirit teaches respect for lawful authority. The volunteer was invited to leave. His clearance as a volunteer was revoked. On another occasion, we had a volunteer who had earned trust and respect from all areas of the prison. That is, until he was discovered to have counterfeited a state identification badge. He claimed that he had made the nearly-perfect badge so he could use it in case he lost his real one. Because his deceit was planned and took much forethought, he was asked to leave.

As a final example, a woman volunteer came in with a church group that had been providing a Sunday afternoon worship service several times a year. Her attire did not lead the mind to religious values. We spoke to the leader of the group, reminding him of his responsibility to see to it that the members of his group promoted the values in keeping with responsible religious expression. The woman was told she did not have the maturity necessary to be a future part of our volunteer team.

In conclusion, while it is true that a lot of time is necessary to train volunteers and coordinate the schedules and paperwork involved with their entry into and exit from the institution, the mere fact that they can multiply our presence and effectiveness with the inmates from five to eight times more than we could do by ourselves, makes the effort worthwhile.

Secondly, taking the time to train new volunteers helps us to be more aware of what it is we are doing for and with the inmates and civilian staff. When we have to explain ourselves to others, it causes us to look directly at what we do and why. Sometimes a question or observation from a volunteer will cause us to take a new look directly at an avenue of ministry we had never thought about before. So their presence helps us to stay alert and fresh to our own personal ministerial style and purpose.

Thirdly, some chaplains worry that the time taken to train and coordinate volunteers could be seen by the administration as "time wasted" by a professional pastor; that the time could be better provided by a lay director of volunteers; that the more volunteers we have, the less a full-time chaplain is needed. The fact is the opposite is true in all cases. The best teacher for this observation is the corps of volunteers themselves. Frequently they remind us that if we were not there for theological and pastoral consultation and guidance, they would not be able to function as well as they do. The questions, needs and problems they are confronted with, and the variety of faith groups we have, could not be handled without extensive training in dogmatic theology, pastoral theology, pastoral counseling, interpretation of sacred writings, religious meditation, religious initiation rites and ceremonies, religious education and sacred liturgy.

Every one of these areas is rightfully the responsibility of, and in the domain of, a well-trained chaplain. As said before, time spent making these areas more effective for the inmates is not time wasted by a professional pastor. The more volunteers we have, the more the institution understands what we and the volunteers are really doing, the more they see that a lay coordinator would not be appropriate for this kind of ministry.

Perhaps life would be simpler today if the chaplaincy could be a one-person operation for only one faith group. Even if a chaplain had the luxury of devoting her full-time attention to one faith group, the sheer numbers of inmates in a faith group, and the complexity of their spiritual needs, and the variety of levels of religious maturity within a group, would seem to make the one-person, one-group rule a practical impossibility in today's world. If a chaplain is going to be true to his pastoral calling, it seems to me he has no choice but to humbly recognize his limitations and the needs of the people entrusted to his spiritual direction. If she is a person of integrity, she has no choice but to reach out to her sisters and brothers in the "outside world" to ask for help. Responsible chaplaincy today, without the existence of volunteers, would be an oxymoron.

EPILOGUE

After working a little more than eighteen years in two state prisons, and in the process of beginning to work in a federal prison, I find myself looking backward as well as forward. Through my professional association with a prayer support group of six pastors, having met for twenty years, and through my regular attendance at professional workshops and conferences and retreats, I hope I have been able to keep the barnacles knocked off the old sloop, as I've tried to sail a course of faith with inmates and civilian staff. It is not easy to avoid being crusty after this long a journey.

In all honesty, it has been more enjoyable, more of the time, working with inmates who are seeking a grounding in faith, than it has been working frequently with civilians, who do not want to journey inward for fear of what they might find. All change is painful. As has been said before, when the pain of change is seen to be less than the pain we are now in, we will change. I hope I have been able to give courage to some to see that the pain of change is worthwhile.

Aside from governors and legislators and denominational leaders, who seldom ever show any real interest in chaplaincy, other than an occasional kudos from off stage, the greatest challenge for a chaplain who is striving to spark a ray of hope in the souls of inmates is the working relationship with so many wardens, deputy wardens and chaplains, who don't have the foggiest notion of what a chaplain does or is supposed to be.

In all honesty, it is at least as much the church's responsibility as it is the state's to demand the highest caliber of service and training from a chaplain. How can the state be expected to know what are decent theological and pastoral standards for chaplaincy, if the church refuses to enter into the dialogue? There should be a council of congregations in every state, with the backing of the highest authorities of those churches, to monitor the training and delivery of pastoral care in all institutional settings. There should be a peer review of every chaplain every year by a highly-trained staff of this council of congregations. They should be endowed with the authority to put a chaplain on probation if he or she fails to meet continuing professional standards. When performance fails to meet standards after a year following probation, the chaplain's endorsement from his or her denomination should be revoked, and the chaplain should be removed. Who else is there to protect the inmates from less than stellar professional conduct? They are in no position to go somewhere else to be spiritually fed.

At the same time that the council of congregations reviews the professional performance of the chaplain, that performance rating should include a review of the professional sensitivity and support of religious services by the civilian leadership of each institution. This evaluation should be sent to the director of the state department of prisons, the governor, the president of the senate and the speaker of the house of representatives. An earnest dialogue must be undertaken by church and state leadership, in order that religion be as professionally respected within the structure of the administration of an institution as are education, psychology, medicine and security.

The recent reality, as I have seen it, is that religion is not taken seriously by far too many wardens, deputy wardens, and central office functionaries. That is not to say that I have not worked with some seriously dedicated men and women of faith. But they really swim upstream to keep a sense of decency and respect about them. I have seen those who strive to recognize inmates as Children of God made fun of or cast aside as though their ideas were of no account. Yet most often these civilians were far more broadly educated than their immediate supervisors.

I do not take pleasure in saying this. But I have visited dozens of prisons, been on committees that have interviewed scores of candidates for chaplaincy positions, and been the president of a chaplain's association that numbered 110 members in 47 institutions in four departments of state government. I visited all their institutions in a two year period. I have met with their civilian supervisors at all levels. I have worked with ten wardens and ten deputy wardens, five state directors, and two state chaplain supervisors. I have been a part-time lobbyist at the statehouse, and dined with three governors. But secular materialistic utilitarianism holds sway over the minds of too many managers to the degree that they seldom have the energy or time to think about the impact of the decisions they make upon the religious life of the institution. As just one brief example, there was a very cordial deputy warden of operations, who made 46 decisions in two years that had a direct impact on the delivery of religious services inside the institution, and never once did he consult a chaplain before making his decisions public policy.

On the other hand, the spiritual life of nearly two million incarcerated citizens of the United States should at least register on the ethical scale of the major denominations. To my knowledge, this has not been addressed in a way that can garner media coverage. How can we expect the existentialistic agnostics, who administer some areas of central office, to appreciate the work of a chaplain?

It is out of my life experience that I have felt the need, not to discourage, condemn or lecture, but to provide an opportunity to explain, challenge and educate. What I have written is not a researched, scholarly work. It is an effort from the heart in which I have tried to offer the fruits of meditation regarding my personal, pastoral experiences. Certainly, and admittedly, I have brought my biases and preferences to this work. It is not without purpose and design that the first two chapters are about servanthood and the ministry of public prayer. Without these priorities, in the order presented, a clergy person does not belong in chaplaincy and probably is unfit for ministry altogether.

Indifferent ignorance costs the taxpayer a fortune and wastes talent. I don't know that a manager gets out of bed with the intention of ignoring the talents and gifts of a chaplain. But to hire a person with 24 years of education from accredited institutions and use those skills less frequently than those of a sergeant, who may have a high school education, seems to defy logic. It makes no sense to hire a professional skilled in human behavior and communication and then put that person in a work environment where sixty percent of the work hours are spent in performing secretarial tasks. The only explanation for such a condition is malice-free, disinterested, indifferent ignorance. It is my hope that this book will challenge administrators to investigate the potential talent that a chaplain has, and to use that talent for the maximum good of the clients whom the chaplain was hired to serve.

Unfortunately, some chaplains are hired without regard to education or skills, some not even having graduated from college. Accredited degrees, pastoral and professional training, even ordination, have been disregarded for some who have been hired.

Such people are being paid for skills they do not have. For the sake of decency and ethical conduct, I hope this book will challenge those chaplains, who are working in this condition to get the certified training they need to perform their ministry.

Administrators, churches, denominational leaders, chaplains — this book is addressed to them all. It does not pretend to be the authoritative, definitive, or exhaustive word or work on chaplaincy. May it not be the last word. For those of you whom this book might excite, enthuse, intrigue or anger, sit down and write your insights, share your opinions, or just sound off. The public for whom we work, and the clients to whom we minister, will be the ultimate benefactors.

"What did you go out into the wasteland to see?" What did you get ordained to be?

This book was designed and published by St. Pauls/ Alba House, the publishing arm of the Society of St. Paul, an international religious congregation of priests and brothers dedicated to serving the Church through the communications media. For information regarding this and associated ministries of the Pauline Family of Congregations, write to the Vocation Director, Society of St. Paul, 7050 Pinehurst, Dearborn, Michigan 48126 or check our internet site, www.albahouse.org